Understanding Spiritual Maturity

DR. C.V. WHITE

UNDERSTANDING SPIRITUAL MATURITY

Copyright @ 2007 Dr. Cynthia V. White

All rights reserved. No part of this book may be reproduced or transmitted in any form or by any means, electronic or mechanical including photocopying, recording, or by any information storage or retrieval system, without written permission from the author.

Unless otherwise quoted all word definitions Greek and Hebrew and scripture quotations are from the King James Version of the Bible as recorded in the Blue Letter Bible: Retrieved from http://www.bluelet-terbible.org. All other scripture quotations from the amplified Bible were retrieved from the biblegateway.com by the Lockman Foundation or International Standard Bible

Encyclopedia, Electronic Database, Copyright © 1995-1996, 2003 by Biblesoft, Inc., All rights reserved, The New Unger's Bible Dictionary-Originally published by Moody Press of Chicago, Illinois, Copyright © 1988.

Published by:
Dr. C.V. White formerly Fruit That Remains LLC
150 Post Office Road
Waldorf, Maryland 20604
Email: drcvwhite@gmail.com

ISBN 13: 978-1-934326-00-8
ISBN 10: 1-934326-00-3

DiViNE Purpose Publishing
www.divinepurposepublishing.com
P. O. Box 906
Branford, CT. 06405

Printed in the United States of America

CONTENTS

Appreciation	5
Dedication	6
Foreword–Prophet Rodney S. Walker, Sr	7
Introduction	10
Chapter One: What it Means to be Spiritually Mature Levels of Spiritual Development	13
Chapter Two: The Babies Level	22
Chapter Three: The Young Children Level	27
Chapter Four: The Young Men Level	31
Chapter Five: The Young Adult Level	35
Chapter Six: The Fathers/Mature Adults Level	39
Chapter Seven: Examples of Spiritual Maturity	44

    Moses, the Deliverer
    The Life of Jacob, the Heel Grabber
    Naomi and Ruth, an Unlikely Pair
    The Young Timothy

Chapter Eight: Commanded to Mature	52

Biblical Terms and Explanations
Salvation

Sanctification
Justification
Adoption
Redemption
Sons of God
Jesus Christ—The SON OF GOD
Spiritual Sonship
The Duty of Sons
Believers Spiritual Growth
Transformation of the Mind
Milk as Spiritual Food
Meat as Spiritual Food
Spiritual Maturity
The Will of God

Chapter Nine: The Timeline for Spiritual Maturity   70

Chapter Ten: Spiritual Maturity, Psychological Age, and Physiological Age   73

Chapter Eleven: What Stunts Spiritual Growth?   87

Summary   92

Additional Quotations   93

Charts and Surveys   98

About the Author   120

Contact Information   123

Bibliography   124

Notes   127

APPRECIATION

I would like to take this opportunity to thank Personally Yours LLC, Bishop Rodney S. Walker, Sr. and Divine Purpose Publishing for their support and assistance in the preparation of this book for publication.

I appreciate your willingness to meet the challenges necessary to complete the final preparation for printing and distribution. Your ideas and suggestions contributed immensely to the success of this project. It was so good to have you as part of the team. I am confident that good things will come from our joint efforts. Thank you, again, for a job well done!

DEDICATION

This book is dedicated my biological father, Rev. Lee Andrew Townes Sr., who helped me to mature naturally and spiritually. My father was an inspiration to me as my father and as my pastor for many years. He started to preach when he was eight years old and continued for seventy-two years. For fifty of those years he pastored churches, and during that time he was instrumental in the spiritual growth of many aspiring pastors and clergy. Also, I thank Bishop Rodney S. Walker, Sr., my spiritual father, who has been instrumental in my spiritual growth. Bishop Walker, I appreciate your support while I was attending school, working, and preparing for ministry. You have been and still are a great blessing to me! Every step of the way you encouraged me to continue with my writing projects. I am appreciative of all of your efforts to assist me in this project and in other areas of my life. I also appreciate God for giving me such a wonderful spiritual father in you! You are a special gift from God and I will always cherish everything that you have poured into me all of these years.

FOREWORD

Dr. White has really tapped into something great by writing this book! Her wonderful manuscript comes to us at a time when the body of Christ has been found lacking in spiritual maturity—a time when our desire to grow has fallen shamefully low on the scale. Growth actually takes a willingness of heart. It does not come by mistake or by waiting; nor does it come if you deny yourself of the proper process. You see, we have reached a place in our lives where God is demanding that we yield to the process of growing. As you read Understanding Spiritual Maturity, you will find that there are several ways to gauge your growth as the author has so skillfully explained.

Dr. White has obviously invested a lot of time in the process of developing this book. It has been uniquely designed to bring people up to the next level of growth. I am persuaded that the only people who will dig into a teaching on this level are those who are serious disciples. The disciples that are mentioned in this book are people who have chosen to give their lives so that they might experience a higher level of spiritual growth and maturity in exchange. As I con- sider all of the many people who I have poured into such as my spiritual daughter, Cynthia, every one of them has had an amazing commitment to the PROCESS—**P**roactive **R**easoning that's **O**pposite active **C**ircumstances and will **E**nhance **S**uccessful **S**essions in real-life experiences.

Most of the people who are in the church grow to a certain level and then begin to die spiritually because they lose consciousness of the whole growth process. They become a part of places that are not able to "grow" them to the next level. When they finally come to themselves they wonder, "How in the world did I get here?" The truth of the matter is that arriving at such a place happens very gradually. It never comes suddenly. You may ask yourself, "Is he talking about me?" No, but I am talking about me. There is no way to understand what that place feels like unless you have actually been there. When I found myself there, I had to kill all of the pride that was in me and go back to the place where I knew I could start growing again. As it is explained in this book, I had to use a gauge by which I could measure where I was with respect to where I should have been at that time. Having determined where I was in my spiritual development, I knew that I had to return to the place where I could further grow and mature. I had no choice but to conclude that without the Word of God, I could not eliminate the ignorance that had kept me bound. The Word tells us in John 8:31-32, "...If ye continue in my word, then are ye my disciples indeed; And ye shall know the truth, and the truth shall make you free." Freedom can come to anyone that commits and submits to the process of growing beyond the circumstances of this life.

If we would ever yield to the life experiences that are designed to teach and mold us in the times that lie ahead, we would totally fulfill the will, call and ministry that God has released to our hands. As we move toward the call as sons into spiritual adoption, allowing God to sanctify us, we will be developed into the kind of disciple that God is looking for in this day. If you desire to be the disciple that God wants to see in this hour, you owe it to yourself to consume every ounce of revelation that exists within the pages of this book. Dr. White has provided you with an extensive, well-researched, biblically sound manual that will assist you as you grow and develop in the things of God. It has now become your responsibility to read it and to rise to the challenge of growing in the Lord! To borrow the words of the Apostle Paul, "I would not have you to be ignorant."

—Bishop Rodney S. Walker, DD.
Founder
Bishop R. S. Walker Ministries
Senior Pastor
Heritage Church International

INTRODUCTION

Maturity has always been a conflicting topic of interest and discussion. Do you remember four-year-old Suzie? Whenever her mother left the bedroom, little Suzie would rush to her vanity, recklessly apply her mother's most expensive foundation and the brightest lipstick she could find, and then proceed to search Mom's closet for those three-inch heels she bought at the red tag sale a few days ago. Never mind the fact that the shoe's heel alone was taller than she was! It didn't even matter that her mother's favorite blouse danced around her ankles, or that Mom's favorite heirloom earrings were so heavy that Suzie could barely lift her head up. Suzie wanted to play "grown-up"!

And what about twelve-year-old Marcus, full of hormones and devoid of any reasonable amount of common sense, who declared with every ounce of defiance a young man his age could muster, "I don't need to wait until I'm sixteen! I can drive right now"? He could barely walk across the street without bumping his head. And then there's the beautiful Tiffany—the "know it all" adolescent who couldn't "wait to turn eighteen and get out of this house so I can do what I want when I want" even though her parents still had to tell her when to wash her clothes and how to wash them. But not one of these persons could have been worse than Ms. Louise who lived down the street, right?

Ms. Louise was always having her 30th birthday even though her driver's license revealed that she was well over 53 years old. She dressed just like the teenagers did and was never spotted without her portable CD player or the latest pair of sneakers. Whenever you addressed her as "Ms. Louise," she insisted that you call her "Lou-Lou" because that's what all of her close friends that were half her age called her.

All of us have known a "Suzie," a "Marcus," a "Tiffany," or a "Lou- Lou," and if the truth were told, we have all been them at one time or another. We have either tried to reach maturity before its time, or we have tried to shun it in its appointed time. Spiritual Maturity is no different. In this book, Understanding Spiritual Maturity, Christians will become acutely aware of their individual responsibility to "grow up" in the things of God. Not only will this book provoke you to mature, it will also show each reader where he or she stands, developmentally, in their Christian walk.

Babies need to know that they are babies. Toddlers need to know that they are toddlers. Adults need to know that they are adults. Neither babies, toddlers, nor adults can decide whether or not they will mature. They simply have no choice in the matter—they will grow. It is not so where spiritual maturity is concerned. If you want to, God will allow you to remain a spiritual infant for as long as you want. No, that's not God's desire, but He allows us the freedom to choose spiritual immaturity if we so desire.

In this book, you will be able to determine where you are in your Christian walk and what victories and pitfalls you should expect with each stage of development. Although this work is Christian in nature, you will also find several theoretical studies that support the various stages of

Spiritual Maturity. Spiritually speaking, are you a baby, a young child, a young man, a young adult, or a spiritual father? As you read this book, you will find the answer to this question and many more questions.

Chapter 1
What it Means to be Spiritually Mature

It would be silly to discuss the various levels of spiritual maturity without first defining the term itself. We have used the term "spiritually mature Christian" so loosely within the body of Christ that it seems to have lost its true meaning. Simply put, a spiritually mature Christian is a person who is led by the Holy Spirit. The word, or expression, describes a person who does not lean to his or her own understanding but, with childlike faith, obeys the Lord without debating and arguing with Him. Spiritually mature Christians will go in whatever direction the Holy Spirit leads, just as trees bend in whatever direction the wind is blowing. Our Christian walk is a partnership with the Holy Spirit, but the Holy Spirit must be the Senior Partner.

Concerning the partnership between our Christian walk and the Holy Spirit, Oswald Sanders, an early twentieth century Christian minister and teacher, offered the following analogy: "Some businesses operate quite successfully with one member being a working partner and the other being a sleeping partner. The latter, though not involved in the day-to-day conduct of the business, makes an essential contribution by providing the capital for the operation. He, of course, shares proportionately in the profits. The Holy Spirit, how- ever, will not consent to be a sleeping partner, although He may be a secret partner in the sense that He is not visible in the partnership business. He must be accorded the role of Senior Partner and have control of the whole enterprise if there is to be a harmonious and successful operation."

It is not enough to know what a spiritually mature Christian is or what spiritually mature means. We must also know how this spiritual maturity is obtained. The Bible talks about growing up, or maturing, in terms of what we are able to eat in regard to the Word of God. The more spiritual food that we eat the more we grow. The more we grow, the more we learn the way and the will of the Lord. The more we learn the will and the way of the Lord, the more we will be like Him. The food of the Lord Jesus Christ helps us to grow up to be like Him. The book of Hebrews gives us an example in chapter 5:12-14 concerning eating spiritual food and growing thereby:

> *"For when for the time ye ought to be teachers, ye have need that one teach you again which be the first principles of the oracles of God; and are become such as have need of milk, and not of strong meat. For every one that useth milk is unskillful in the word of righteousness: for he is a babe."*
>
> Hebrews 5:12-13

These passages let us know that Christians who continue to need the basics and are unable to discern good from evil are still babies. This becomes the first characteristic of a baby Christian. Let's continue on to the 14th verse:

> *"But strong meat belongeth to them that are of full age, even those who by reason of use have their senses exercised to discern both good and evil."*
>
> Hebrews 12:14

Being able to discern good from evil becomes the first characteristic of a Christian adult.

Now that we've answered the "what?" and "how?" of spiritual maturity, we must answer the "why?" Why are we encouraged, as sons of God, to be mature? One of the reasons we are encouraged, as sons of God, to be mature is very simple and uncomplicated: God wants His children to be mature because He is. In fact, Jesus admonished the same in Matthew 5:48 (Amplified Bible) when He said, "You, therefore, must be perfect [growing into complete maturity of godliness in mind and character, having reached the proper height of virtue and integrity], as your heavenly Father is perfect."

In the same way, "No one knows the thoughts of God except the Spirit of God (NIV)." This is why we as believers are encouraged to mature. God wants us to be like Him, "mature," and when we grow up and become mature He can share with us information, revelation and a portion of the deep things of God. Babies and immature children cannot handle the pressure of persecution, suffering and affliction associated with receiving this information, revelation in the fullness of what God desires for those who love him.

The instructions given to believers in the passages before Matthew 5:48 and after are difficult to accomplish if we are not mature. When Jesus commands believers to "Love your enemies," many of us respond to His instruction as if we are hard of hearing: "What?" "You want me to love my enemies?" We then go on to tell God how our enemies have harmed us and why we should not be told to love them. What we are really seeking is God's sympathy.

Our enemies are not always unbelievers, sometimes they are our very own siblings (our sisters and brothers in Christ). Whether the enemy is an unbeliever or a believer, one thing is certain: God will not kill any of His children at the request of another. Mature Christians are expected to love their enemies and to not wish for their deaths. It is not possible to obey God in areas like this if you are not perfect (mature). God commands us to grow to maturity so that we can love our enemies and become an expression of His love in the earth.

We are greatly encouraged by the Word of God to mature. This can also be seen in the book of Hebrews. The author, in the 1st verse of the 6th chapter writes, "Therefore leaving the principles of the doc- trine of Christ, let us go on unto perfection; not laying again the foundation of repentance from dead works, and of faith toward God." The word "perfection" comes from the Greek word "teleioteta," which means "full growth." We see the same word, "perfection," in Luke 8:14-15: "And that which fell among thorns are they, which, when they have heard, go forth, and are choked with cares and riches and pleasures of this life, and bring no fruit to perfection. But that on the good ground are they, which in an honest and good heart, having heard the word, keep it, and bring forth fruit with patience." As we read these verses of scripture, we can see that we are encouraged, again, to grow up and bring forth fruit. The word "perfection" in this context is the Greek word "telesphoreo" (tel-es-for-eh'-o), which means to be a bearer to completion (maturity), i.e. to ripen fruit (figuratively): bring fruit to perfection.
While Christians are encouraged to grow, it does take

time. As babies, we start fast but eventually we slow down and continue grow- ing at a slower pace. The good news is that God will complete everything that He starts in us—He is not intimidated by time!

"It seems that most believers have difficulty in realizing and facing up to the inexorable fact that God does not hurry in his development of our Christian life. He is working from and for eternity! So many feel they are not making progress unless they are swiftly and constantly forging ahead. Now it is true that the new con- vert often begins and continues for some time at a fast rate. But this will not continue if there is to be healthy growth and ultimate maturity. God Himself will modify the pace.[2]"
Maturity is important in both the Christian and secular environment. Each of these groups spends a large amount of time trying to get people to grow up naturally and spiritually. Take a look at some of the things Christian and secular authors are saying about maturity from *Draper's Book of Quotations for the Christian World*[3]:

> 'Tis a mark of great perfection to bear with the imperfections of others.
> **_ITALIAN PROVERB_**

> God never destroys the work of his own hands, he removes what would pervert it, that is all. Maturity is the stage where the whole life has been brought under the control of God.
>
> **_OSWALD CHAMBERS (1874–1917)_**

> In the early stages of our Christian experience we are inclined to hunt in an overplus of delight for

the commandments of our Lord in order to obey them out of our love for him, but when that conscious obedience is assimilated and we begin to mature in our life with God, we obey his commandments unconsciously, until in the maturest stage of all we are simply children of God through whom God does his will, for the most part unconsciously to us.

OSWALD CHAMBERS (1874–1917)

Maturity begins to grow when you can sense your concern for others outweighing your concern for yourself.

JOHN MACNAUGHTON

Maturity is the ability to be comfortable with people who are not like us.

VIRGIL A. KRAFT

One of the marks of spiritual maturity is the quiet confidence that God is in control . . . without the need to understand why he does what he does.

CHARLES R. SWINDOLL (1934–)

The spheres God brings us into are not meant to teach us something but to make us something.

OSWALD CHAMBERS (1874–1917)

The stronger and deeper the roots, the less visible they are.

CHARLES R. SWINDOLL (1934–)

There are no shortcuts to spiritual maturity. It takes time to be holy.

ERWIN W. LUTZER (1941–)

Why stay we on earth except to grow?

ROBERT BROWNING (1812–1889)

One direct result of growing up in the things of God is an increase in spirituality. Since we've examined what Christian and secular authors are saying about maturity, why not examine some of the things Christian authors are saying about spirituality, also from *Draper's Book of Quotations for the Christian World* [4]?

> A vessel that grows as it is filled will never be full. If a bin able to hold a cartload grew while you were dumping your load in it, you could never fill it. The soul is like that: the more it wants, the more it is given; the more it receives, the more it grows.

MEISTER ECKHART (C. 1260–C. 1327)

He who believes himself to be far advanced in the spiritual life has not even made a good beginning.

JEAN PIERRE CAMUS (1584–1652)

Many people think that a "spiritual Christian" is mystical, dreamy, impractical, and distant. When he prays, he shifts his voice into a sepulchral tone in tremolo. This kind of unctuous piety is a poor example of true spirituality. To be "spiritually minded" simply means to look at earth from heaven's point of view. The spiritually minded believer makes his decisions on the basis of eternal values and not the passing fads of society.

WARREN W. WIERSBE (1929–)

Our intellect and other gifts have been given to be used for God's greater glory, but sometimes they become the very god for us. That is the saddest part: we are losing our balance when this happens. We must free ourselves to be filled by God. Even God cannot fill what is full.

MOTHER TERESA OF CALCUTTA (1910–)

Spiritual maturity: the quiet confidence that God is in control.

CHARLES R. SWINDOLL (1934–)

True spirituality manifests itself in:
1. The desire to be holy rather than happy
2. The desire to see the honor of God advanced through his life
3. The desire to carry his cross
4. The desire to see everything from God's viewpoint
5. The desire to die right rather than live wrong
6. The desire to see others advance at his expense
7. The desire to make eternity-judgments instead of time-

A. W. TOZER (1897–1963)

Levels of Spiritual Development

Having taken a closer look at both maturity and spirituality, we are now ready to name and discuss the five levels of spiritual development. Those levels of development are the *Baby Level*, which includes those Christians who are spiritually from birth to one year of age; the *Young Children Level*, which encompasses Christians who are spiritually between the ages of one through two years; the *Young Men Level*, which depicts spiritually adolescent and teenage Christians from two to four years of spiritual age; the *Young Adults Level*, where persons are slightly more mature at four through ten years of spiritual age; and, finally, the *Fathers Level*, which is comprised of spiritually mature adults whose spiritual age contains the broadest range of years, ten to twenty years.

Chapter 2
The Babies Level

The first and least mature of these groups of Christians is the Babies Level. This particular group of people is heavily dependent upon the pastor and the elders of the church. They need constant feed- ing of the basics of their salvation and constant reinforcement of spiritual direction. At this level, they are just being introduced to the Bible which contains what is called "the oracles of God."

"The word 'oracle' literally means 'the speaking place.' Christianity arises out of a faith in an infinite, personal God who has not been silent, but has spoken. The Bible is indeed the oracle of God, His speaking place.[5]"

The oracles of God simply translate as "the written Word of God." Babies lack spiritual knowledge because they have not had the opportunity to develop the skills needed to study the written Word of God (His logos voice), or they have not taken the opportunity to study His logos word (the person of Jesus Christ, who is the Word of God according to John 1:1).

"Logos" is a Greek word that means "the Word." According to Unger's Illustrated Bible Dictionary, it is a term used by the Apostle John conveying, most expressively, the mission of Jesus as the revealer of the Godhead (John 1:1,14). The title declares Christ's eternity and absolute deity ("In the beginning was the Word, and...the Word was God"), as well as His assumption of humanity for man's salvation ("and the

Word became flesh"). Words are the vehicle for the revelation of the thoughts and intents of the mind to others. In the Person of the Incarnate Logos, God made Himself fully known to man. Nothing knowable by man, concerning God, is undisclosed by incarnate deity. Christ, as the Word, constitutes the complete and ultimate divine revelation. God has spoken with finality in "His Son" (Hebrews 1:1-2).

So, we see that those at the Baby Level have not yet reached a place of fully knowing "logos," neither have they reached a place of knowing the "rhema" word of God. Taken partially from the *International Standard Bible Encyclopedia, Electronic Database*, the "rhema" word of God is defined as a word that God is speaking *now*. It is considered to be a word in itself. "Logos," on the other hand, is a spoken word with general reference to what is in the speaker's mind.

Babies in Christ are newborns. Just as newborn babies in the natural, babies in Christ are not able to discern good from evil. They are self-centered and focused only on eating and taking in whatever they need to learn and grow. At this stage, most of what they take in goes right through them because they need constant teaching and nurturing to deal with the attacks of the devil and to overcome old habits and practices. Typically, babies do not have the interest of the church or the people in the church as a high priority in their lives. Remember, they are self-centered at this point, and everything is about them. At this juncture or moment in time, they are only able to have faith for themselves. All they care about is Jesus because they realize that it is He who has saved them. They will also need the spiritual adults in the church (pastors) who serve as fathers, elders who serve as mentors, and mothers, fathers, aunts, uncles, and others, all of whom are their sisters and brothers, to plan, protect and provide for them as they grow spiritually.

Many times people who are still babies in Christ find themselves in positions of leadership for various reasons. This causes a serious problem because as babies, they are not able to serve others. Anyone who is still a baby is still looking to be served. They are not ready to take on the responsibility of serving others if that means taking the attention away from themselves.

"Spiritual maturity is indispensable to good leadership. A novice or new convert should not be pushed into leadership. A plant needs time to take root and come to maturity, and the process cannot be hurried. The seed must take root downward before it can bear fruit upward. J.A. Bengle says that novices usually have 'an abundance of [vegetation]' and are not yet pruned by the cross." In 1 Timothy 3:10, referring to qualifications for deacon, Paul urges, "They must first be tested."[6]

Because babies do not yet know good from evil (Hebrews 5:12), they are more in touch with the things of the flesh than they are with spiritual things. However, they have great zeal for the Lord. They are literally ready to go out and save the world! They love the Lord and are very excited about being in the family of God.

Although they are zealous, excited, and love the Lord, babies cannot be expected to be strong in the righteousness of the Lord since they are just beginning to understand the Word of God. At this point they are not necessarily interested in growing up to be like Jesus Christ; they are just glad that He is God!

Another interesting fact about those at the Baby Level of development is that they believe that all church people should follow Jesus. They are also very vulnerable to abuse and misuse at the hands of other immature Christians. Because of this fact, many of them leave the church with a bitter taste in their mouths because of their disappointment with the congregation at large or with church leadership. As they grow, however, they will learn that the church is a hospital for sick souls and a rehabilitation center for recovering sinners.

Bill Bright, the author of Handbook for Christian Maturity, writes that the personal emphasis of this group is that they exercise their faith for their own benefit. Although each individual is uniquely different, there are several characteristics that are prevalent among these immature Christians.

Like it or not, Christians at this level of spiritual maturity (0-1 year of spiritual age) get away with more things than any other group. As we've always guessed, God loves babies with a special love. He will wink at what they are doing because He knows that they are too young to even understand what it is they are actually doing. Some additional characteristics of this age level are:

- Their sins have been forgiven. (1 John 12-13)
- They focus their thoughts on evil, because they are ignorant of the deeper truths of God's word, and of the evil one (Satan) and his tactics. (1 Corinthians 14:20)
- They are just coming into the knowledge of God to *really know Him*. (1 John 2:12)
- They have overcome the world. (1 John 2:17)

- They only know the basics of the word. (Hebrews 5:14) and
- They have major struggles with their flesh. (1 Corinthians 3:2-3) Being a baby has benefits, but someday, one has to grow up.

Chapter 3
The Young Children Level

Leaving the *Babies Level*, the next level of spiritual development is the *Young Children Level*. Unlike those found in the previous level of spiritual development, young children are no longer focused on themselves, but have now become interested in their peers, too. They look around the church trying to fit in and desperately want to be part of a church family. This is a very critical time for those persons at this level because they begin to lean on their own understanding. Their spiritual walk begins to seem tough because the way of the Lord is to hate all evil, albeit the world that we live in is evil. They have not yet reached the stage where they know that they are "in this world, but not of this world." They struggle as friends, family, and others begin to try to pull them back into the world.

This is also a time when they will have to choose between the way of the Lord, which is the correct way, or the way of the world, which is the way of Satan. Because most of the things that feel good to us are not good for us, choosing what is good for us becomes harder and harder to do; so it is for these "young children."

Peer pressure is hard to overcome. Once people begin to say things like "It doesn't take all of that," "Surely God knew you were like that when you were saved," "God is probably okay with whatever comes to your mind to do," or "Oh, come on, telling one lie won't hurt, besides you will get in trouble if you tell the truth," to young children in Christ it becomes very difficult for them to discern the proper perspective to place these types of comments and statements. These types of statements will cause young children to want to say "yes" while yielding to the peer pressure of the worldly and sometimes carnal attitudes of the unsaved or babies in Christ, friends, family members, or business associates. At this point in time they are more concerned with the approval of men than they are with the approval of God.

Although they are spiritually young children, they are not with- out direction. God will speak to them through the preached and the taught Word during Sunday worship services, at Sunday school, at Bible study, or at other church school programs. However, other voices will also speak to them—voices of their own flesh and from the enemy, namely Satan.

At this level, these persons will also need the spiritual adults of the church to lead and guide them as they learn to listen to God. Of course they will make many mistakes as they attempt to hear God because the voices that are not of God are able to sound just like Him. Satan is the great imitator. Because of this, it is absolutely necessary that these young children are taught to know the ways of the Lord so they will know what God will or will not do and what He will or will not say.

This stage of spiritual development is when God begins to teach. Once individuals reach this level, God ceases to help them as much as He did when they were babies. He gives them ample teaching through the pastor and Christian Education. After they receive this teaching, God will then stand back to see what they are going to do with what they have learned. If they happen to get it right, they will move on to the next lesson. If they don't get it right, God's love will correct and admonish them to get it right the next time.

Most often, Christians who fall into this category are found entertaining filthiness, silly talk, and coarse jesting, all of which are not fitting for believers, and they are unaware that they should be giving thanks for all things (Ephesians 5:4). Seeing that they are not yet fully mature, they may also allow immorality, impurity or greed to be named among them (Ephesians 5:3) as they walk as the Gentiles walk, in the vanity of their minds—struggling with their flesh (Ephesians 4:17). Having fashioned themselves according to the for- mer lusts in their ignorance (1 Peter 1:14), they will need to be reminded that they have become and are now children of the light and no longer children of darkness (Ephesians 5:7.8).

Even as young children in the natural, this group of believers may also succumb to the wiles of deception. Characteristically, they may be deceived by the empty words of unbelievers, not realizing that the wrath of God comes upon the sons of disobedience or unbelievers (Ephesians 5:6). Because of their immaturity, they are subject to what Ephesians 4:14 describes as being *"tossed to and fro, and carried about with every wind of doctrine, by the sleight of men, and cunning craftiness, whereby they lie in wait to deceive."*

As stated earlier, these one- and two-year-olds are given direction through and by the preached and taught Word of God; however, they still need to learn what is pleasing to the Lord and what is not. For example, they may not know for certain that no immoral or impure person or covetous man, who is an idolater, has an inheritance in the kingdom of Christ and God (Ephesians 5:5). Yes, they have progressed from the Babies Level, but sadly, there are still in a state of ignorance and of intellectual darkness (Matthew 11:16). In contrast to this intellectual darkness, they need to be taught that the fruit of the light that exists in all goodness and righteousness and truth.

In today's society, when we think of adolescents, teenagers and young men, a myriad of thoughts enters our minds: reckless, rebellious, and rowdy, just to name a few. But if we would look beyond our judgmental minds, we would realize that the most accurate and descriptive word for this group of people is "transitional." This is also true of spiritual adolescents and teenagers.

Chapter 4
The Young Men Level

The *Young Men Level* is comprised of believers who have learned enough of the Word of God and the work of God to go to another spiritual level in Him, but they are uncertain about whether or not they really want to go. They are no longer young children and are making the *transition* into hearing God for themselves. They are ready to be teenagers, but they know that the shift is going to cost them something.

As spiritual adolescents and teenagers, they begin to give up things that they held so dear such as going out "clubbing" every weekend. This stage of development requires that they give up some of their social activities that they shared with their lifelong friends and family members. This is a time of choosing God over things, people, idols, and self. It is not an easy time, but when one chooses God first, the reward is great! When they are able to make this kind of decision, they will move on to the turbulent teen level.

The turbulent teen level can prove to be the most difficult level of all. At this level of development, this group wants to be in the place where there is action. They have outgrown the need just to be accepted and now want to be a part of what is happening in the church. This process of transition, however, must be recognized by the leadership of the church in order to facilitate an easy conversion to the next level of growth. This progression can be easily observed as the desire to accomplish everything quickly manifests itself.

Just as you and I desired when we were teenagers, spiritual adolescents and teenagers at this level begin wanting to become independent of the adults in the church. At this place in spiritual development, it is difficult to submit to authority because they want to be the authority.

To add to their independent spirits, those who fall in this category are somewhat headstrong. For instance, they're not particularly concerned about whether or not they are spiritually or naturally prepared to do the jobs they've been assigned because they are convinced that they no longer need any direction or guidance from the leadership of the church. They are fearless and confident about everything. In fact, they are convinced that they know everything that needs to be known—they are the famed "Know It All Group." They believe that they are ready for anything! But, their fearlessness and confidence is misplaced because it is based on perceptions and not reality.

Even though these traits may seem a bit annoying and bother- some, it is essentially a common route to becoming an adult. Young men must first practice before they actually get the job. This is a time when they can function as an adult without all of the responsibilities of adulthood. The adults in the church are able to give them more responsibility while providing a safety net to catch them when they make mistakes due to immaturity and a lack of knowledge.

This is an exciting time for growing and learning! All of the spiritual sense that is learned will assist them in their transition to the next level of spiritual growth. When these maturing Christians begin choosing God over everything else, even when it becomes difficult but rewarding to do so, they will find that the reward of putting Him first is greater than anything that can be imagined by the human mind.

Many choices have been made from the beginning of being born again to this level. We will not always choose the way of the Lord during the growing process, but the Lord will never leave us as we progress to being like Him. But at whatever point we are ready to transition to the next level, we can be sure that we have made enough godly choices to be promoted to the next stage of development. We must always remember that promotion comes from God; we cannot promote ourselves.

The *Young Men Level* displays several pictures of the advancement to maturity. In contrast to the previous levels, those who find themselves at this stage of development refuse to participate in the unfruitful deeds of darkness, acknowledge that it is even disgraceful to speak of those things that are done by them in secret, and even expose those who do these unfruitful deeds of darkness. In fact, they are mature enough to know that all things become visible when they are exposed by the light, for everything that becomes visible is light (Ephesians 5:11-13)

Naturally, adolescents and teenagers are in search of their own identity. They want to create something that is uniquely theirs—it may be a particular style, a specific swagger, or a peculiar laugh. It is no different in the spiritual realm. Spiritual adolescents and teenagers are careful as to how they walk—not with a pimp or a stride—but with care, not walking as unwise men, but as wise men (Ephesians 5:15). At the same moment, they are cognizant of their future and make the most of their time, knowing that the days are evil (Ephesians 5:16). They are not foolish, but they do understand what the will of the Lord is (Ephesians 5:17).

Lastly, most of these two- to four-year-old Christians are at the place where they are able to practice self-control. Temptation visits every man, woman, boy and girl. But at this stage, believers are able to resist it. They are no longer foolish, but they understand what the will of the Lord is (Ephesians 5:17). Moreover, Ephesians 5:18 gives us a wonderful example of people at this level who do not get drunk with wine, but are filled with the Spirit. This level of development also helps to better both vertical and horizontal relationships. Vertically, it is typical of this group to always give thanks to the Father for all things in the name of our Lord Jesus Christ (Ephesians 5:20). Horizontally, a spiritual respect is fostered among fellow brethren.

They speak to one another in psalms and hymns and spiritual songs, singing and making melody with their heart to the Lord and are subject to one another in the fear of Christ (Ephesians 5:19, 20).

Chapter 5
The Young Adult Level

The final transition before reaching the mature adult level (Fathers) takes place at the Young Adult Level. At this level believers begin making God a priority in their lives. They begin to focus on what God wants and what makes Him happy. When they have progressed to this level of development, they have decided to put God at the very top of the list. God becomes more and more a part of their everyday lives, so much so that they begin to seek Him in a more intimate way. Having such a desire to know God more deeply, these "young adults" begin to ask questions of their pastors or spiritual leaders like "What is it that God has called me to do?", "How do I begin doing what He wants me to do?", and "What part of the body of Christ am I in this local church or in the church universal? An Arm? A leg? An eye?" Asking these questions is an easy thing to do, but once the answers are given and received, these "almost Fathers" find that it is not as easily done as it is said. They desperately desire to be obedient to the Lord, but fail to realize that they can't be obedient without the Holy Spirit. This is the first lesson that must be learned.

At this particular place, Christians begin to seek God for answers that God intends for them to get from their spiritual leader (father, pastor, etc.). The method of God's teaching at this level is to "go see a man ["man" being a generic term for male or female] who is more mature than you whom I have directed to teach and lead you in this specific point of development in your spiritual life." An example of this is found in Acts 9:5-14 in the conversations between Saul, later known as Paul, and God, and between God and Ananias. When God knocked Saul off of his donkey, He had Saul's undivided attention. At this point, God could have restored Saul's sight and told him exactly what He wanted him to do. But, God didn't give Saul any further direction. He simply told Saul to go into the city and that he would be told what to do. God then told Ananias to go to Saul and to restore his sight. From this example, we can clearly see that God's order is facilitated through and by the men and women whom He has chosen to lead and feed. This is the beginning of learning to depend on the Holy Spirit to do what cannot be done by man alone.

In addition to making God a priority and seeking answers from Him, many people who are in this class or category of believers begin to question God about their ability to do what God has purposed for them to do. For instance, the pastor may ask them to teach Sunday school, or to serve in some capacity of the church's infrastructure, and they find that they have no experience for the position they have been given. Now frustrated, they begin to question God and church leadership. They were expecting to get a job that they already knew how to do, because they were expecting to do it themselves—in and of their own power—from within their comfort zone; but God knows that they cannot grow in a comfortable place. Because of this, they must be given something that God knows they can do only with His help. Ultimately, this is what God wants. It forces them to grow by trusting God instead of themselves. When they finally accomplish the task, they acknowledge that God deserves and gets all of the credit, the glory, and the praise. They are now ready to move in the things of God as God begins to teach them more difficult things such as loving people who are their enemies. They come to learn how to do these things in "the uncomfortable place." Loving your enemy is an uncomfortable idea, but how can you minister the love of God to someone you hate and be comfortable?

This level will serve to give persons a more tangible view of our Lord. At this stage, Jesus becomes real, and He is no longer an intellectual idea! Yes, because we are born-again believers, we already know that Jesus died for our sins; but at this stage of development, we know it with more intensity. At this level, Christians realize that Jesus died for the sins of all—even those that did not love Him (his enemies). He said at the point of His death as noted in Luke 23:34, "Father, for- give them, for they do not know what they are doing" (NIV). Even as Jesus desires, not only do Christians know that Jesus died for our sins, but they realize that He died for the sins of everybody, even for those that have not yet made Him their choice and for those that may never make Him their choice. Therefore, we should not think more highly of ourselves than we ought by not considering how much he loves those who are not yet saved. It does not matter what they have done, or what they are doing, He loves them just as much as He loves us. Sometimes this is very difficult to accept since we tend to judge others by what we see, and we want to be judged by our intentions.

This level, the "Young Adult Level," is the where we begin to live a lifestyle of loving the Lord with all of our hearts, minds, and souls, and loving our neighbors as ourselves—a necessary requirement as we prepare to transition into mature adulthood (fathers).

Generally, believers at this stage of development display certain unique traits of maturity that may not be seen at other levels of growth. Among those traits are the desires for sanctification, peace, servanthood, and camaraderie amidst the brethren as seen in 2 Timothy 2:21-26:

> *"If a man therefore purge himself from these, he shall be a vessel unto honour, sanctified, and meet for the master's use, and prepared unto every good work. Flee also youthful lusts: but follow righteous- ness, faith, charity, peace, with them that call on the Lord out of a pure heart. But foolish and unlearned questions avoid, knowing that they do gender strifes. And the servant of the Lord must not strive; but be gentle unto all men, apt to teach, patient, In meekness instructing those that oppose themselves; if God peradventure will give them repentance to the acknowledging of the truth; And that they may recover themselves out of the snare of the devil, who are taken captive by him at his will."*

Although these young adults have the Word of God abiding in them, are strong, and are able to overcome the wicked one (1 John 2:14), they still need to be reminded to speak the truth in love (Ephesians 4:15). Even though they desire to walk in the power of the Lord, they are not yet ready to share in the fellowship of His sufferings (Philippians 3:10).

Chapter 6
The Fathers/Mature Adults Level

Making the transition from spiritual infancy to spiritual maturity often seems to be a difficult, arduous task. Truthfully, traveling down this road does require determination, stamina, and intestinal fortitude or just plain guts. But we will see, as we explore the next and final stage of spiritual development—the Fathers/Mature Adults Level— that the journey is well worth taking!

Fathers are very important in the body of Christ. The term "father," in this context, is not a gender assignment. The term rep- resents a mature person, male or female, that is in a position of fathering the people of God. Many times these are the people who are the pastors or set gifts of a particular house or local assembly. They father the congregation. They become the persons from whom spiritual direction and guidance flows to the people in their charge. What is absolutely essential to know, as we consider fathers, is that one can be a father without being a pastor, but one should not be a pastor without being a father. The father and son relationship is the order of God.

We see an example of this relationship when Paul wrote to the Corinthians concerning their behavior. He reminded them that though they may have ten thousand instructors, they did not have many fathers (1 Corinthians 4:14:17). Paul was their father, and he knew that it was because of God's plan (and His grace) that he held that position. He told them as much in 1 Corinthians 15:9-10:

> *"For I am the least of the apostles, that am not meet to be called an apostle, because I persecuted*

the church of God. But by the grace of God I am what I am: and his grace which was bestowed upon me was not in vain; but I laboured more abundantly than they all: yet not I, but the grace of God which was with me."

In 1 Corinthians 4:14-17 the Apostle Paul shows the Corinthian church the way out of their dilemma. Paul reminds them to become his followers, since he is their father in the gospel. He speaks to them as sons and sent his son in the Lord, Timothy, to bring them into remembrance of this fact, as noted in 1 Corinthians 4:17, "For this reason I am sending to you Timothy, my son whom I love, who is faithful in the Lord. He will remind you of my way of life in Christ Jesus, which agrees with what I teach everywhere in every church (NIV)." Paul knew who he was and why he was given his place in God. However, the Corinthian church was not receiving Paul's fatherhood and had no true father to follow. As long as a congregation or ministry remains out of God's order, the people will experience disorder and lack identity. If we are without a father, then we have no name, no identity, no heritage, no inheritance, and no true brethren.

The order of God within His kingdom is the order of father and son. Paul writes to a chaotic charismatic culture as a father to sons and sends Timothy as a model of what a son in the ministry is really like. The apostle then says that this is part of his "ways, which be in Christ, as I teach every where in every church." If we are ever going to find our way out of this confusion, we have to find God's ways in the kingdom.7 Is there a better reason for maturing to this level? Some of us must become fathers.

At this level, a ten- to fifteen-year process of becoming elders indeed is begun. Christians at this level know that they have to depend upon the Holy Spirit for everything. They decide to lower themselves and lift up Christ Jesus in their lives. By now they know that they must be led by the Holy Spirit in order to function in the resurrection of His Power.

Fathers' lives become living epistles. People begin to want to be like them. Others who witness the lives of these fathers gain confidence that what they thought could not be done is actually functioning in this person. "Surely, if God would do this for them, He will do it for me," they reason.

After a decade of development or a few years more, this group begins to level off and continue to grow higher and higher in the things of the Lord. Many times we will hear people say something about remembering the old saints of the church, "They really trust God," or "They really pray some powerful prayers," etc., not realizing that they are becoming the saints of old. In fact, some have already become the old saints even though they are not old in age.

One thing to remember is that being an old saint grounded in the Lord has nothing to do with age. Even though most of the time we are old when we reach that point, some may reach that point at a young age because God wants to use them early or because they may have a teachable spirit and decided, at an early age, to grow up and not fight the process.

This group is family-centered. They see the church as their family. They remember what Jesus said in Matthew 12:50: "For whosoever shall do the will of my Father which is in heaven, the same is my brother, and sister, and mother." As a result, they have a very high tolerance for every individual in the church.

In their hearts they are sold out to Christ and do not mind making whatever sacrifice that is needed in order for the Gospel to go forward. In fact, they become offerings and sacrifices unto God, themselves, for someone else, or for the gospel's sake as they walk in love, just as Christ also loved them (Ephesians 5:2).

At this particular level of growth, Fathers/Mature Adults (spiritual ages ten through twenty years) have a real sense of who they are and who Jesus is. They know that no matter where their earthly birth- places may be, their true citizenship is in heaven (Philippians 3:20). As fathers, they place no confidence in the flesh, and count all worldly accomplishments such as money, education, prestige, and social class as loss for the sake of Christ (Philippians 3:3,7).

Arriving at this place of maturity requires not only sacrifice, but it also requires the desire to walk in the power of His resurrection and sharing in the fellowship of His sufferings (Philippians 3:10). In addition, Christians who are in this small group of people must learn to forget what is behind them and press toward the goal to win the prize for which God has called them (Philippians 3:15).

Fathers, typically speaking, have reached a level that allows them to be teachers of the Word of God (Hebrews

5:12) and they reproduce themselves regularly (Galatians 4:19; I Corinthians 4:15-16; Philippians 3:17). Because they are actually "fathers/mature adults," we can safely say that they have known God for a long time and have known Him through experience (1 John 2:13-14). They enjoy an intimate relationship with Christ and have a great desire to be like Him.

Each level of spiritual maturity and development, the *Baby Level*, the *Young Children Level*, the *Young Men Level*, the *Young Adults Level*, and the *Fathers/Mature Adults Level* has its own unique pros and cons and its own unique advantages and disadvantages; yet, succeeding at each level is just as important as progressing to the next one. Every step must be taken and mastered before reaching the next level of progression.

Chapter 7
Examples of Spiritual Maturity

A basic spiritual truth to remember at this point is that spiritual growth is facilitated by being as the young in physical age. In spiritual maturity, the oldest shall be like the youngest (Luke 22:26-28). In comparison to natural human development, maturity is closely associated with physical age. The biblical account of the life of Moses gives us a clear example of how spiritual growth is facilitated.

Moses, the Deliverer

Moses knew, after he became an adult, that he was going to be used to save his people; but, he did not have the maturity to know when, where, or how, because he did not yet have a relationship with God. As a result, at forty years old (Acts 7:23) Moses resolved to cast in his lot with his brethren (Hebrews 11:24-26). Having observed an Israelite being beaten by an Egyptian, and thinking that they were alone, Moses killed the Egyptian and buried the corpse in the sand. The next day he endeavored to act as a peacemaker between two Hebrews, but his offer was refused and he became aware that his act of the preceding day was known. It became evident to him that safety was to be found only in flight (Exodus 2:11-15).

How old was Moses, spiritually, at this point? This is a question that is illustrated in the growth chart. It took Moses an additional forty years to reach the maturity level that he needed in order to get to the place where the Lord would be able to use him as a deliverer for the people. Moses had to mature to the adulthood level of spiritual maturity in order to do what God had called him to do.

The Life of Jacob, the Heel Grabber

Another example is found in the life of Jacob. According to Nelson's Illustrated Bible Dictionary, Jacob was one of the twin sons of Isaac and Rebekah. The brother of Esau, Jacob was born in answer to his father's prayer (Genesis 25:21), but he became the favorite son of his mother (Genesis 25:28). He was nicknamed Jacob because, at the birth of the twins, "his hand took hold of Esau's heel," as recorded in Genesis 25:26. According to the accounts in Genesis, Jacob continued to "take hold of" the possessions of others—his brother's birthright (25:29-34), his father's blessing (27:1-29), and his father- in-law's flocks and herds (30:25-43; 31:1).

We can see from this brief account of a portion of Jacob's life that he focused on himself in most of his family relationships. This means that he was not very mature in the ways of the Lord. Fortunately, this fact changed as he became more acquainted with God.

Jacob began his spiritual growth at Bethel when he left the family home in Beersheba to travel to Haran (a city in Mesopotamia), the residence of his uncle, Laban (Genesis 28:10). On the way, as he stopped for the night at Bethel, Jacob had a dream of a staircase reaching from earth to heaven with angels upon it and the Lord above it. He was impressed by the words of the Lord, which promised him inheritance of the land, descendants "as the dust of the earth" in number, and His divine presence. Jacob dedicated the site as a place of worship, calling it Bethel (literally, House of God). More than twenty years later, Jacob returned to this spot, and reached another level in his spiritual growth. At Bethel he built an altar and called the place El Bethel (literally, God of the house of God), and received the divine blessing (35:6-15).

The experience at the ford of the River Jabbok occurred as Jacob returned from his long stay at Haran. While preparing for a reunion with his brother, Esau, of whom he was still afraid (Genesis 32:7), he had a profound event that left him changed in both body and spirit.

Jacob's experience lets us know that growing up in the things of God is going to be a struggle. At the ford of the Jabbok, "Jacob was left alone." (Genesis 32:24). It was night, and he found himself suddenly engaged in a wrestling match in the darkness. This bout lasted until the breaking of the dawn, leaving the socket of Jacob's hip out of joint as he struggled with this mysterious stranger; but he refused to release his grip until he was given a blessing. For the first time in the narrative of Genesis, Jacob had been unable to defeat an opponent. When asked to identify himself in the darkness, he confessed that he was Jacob— the heel- grabber.

Nevertheless, Jacob's struggling earned him a new name! For his struggle "with God and with men," in which he had prevailed, his name was changed to "Israel" (literally, Prince with God). In return, he gave a name to the spot that marked the change. It was to be called "Peniel"—"For I have seen God face to face, and my life is pre- served" (Genesis 32:30). Jacob's spiritual growth caused him to receive a new name. How many

Christians get a new name when they grow up in God? Some were before called "liars," but are now called "people of truth and integrity." Some were before called "thieves" and "robbers," but when they grew up in Christ, their names were changed to "heroes and 'do-gooders'." Some were even called "tale- bearers" before, but when they matured in the ways of the Lord, they were called "confidential peace holders."

Ruth and Naomi, an Unlikely Pair

Another example of spiritual growth is shown in the life story of Ruth and Naomi. Ruth and Naomi began young in their trust of the Lord, but they grew up to become giants in their spiritual growth. Their rise to spiritual maturity gives all of us hope.

Naomi, her husband, Elimelech, and their two sons moved from Bethlehem in Judah to the land of Moab. In Moab, Naomi and Elimelech's two sons were married. It was also in Moab that these same two sons and their father, Elimelech, died. Naomi and Ruth received great blessings from God, but they had to go through a growing process before they were able to receive all that God had for them. As far as Naomi was concerned, she was going home to die; but God meant good for her life. She wasn't aware of His plan in the beginning, but as she grew up in the things of God, she learned to trust Him more. We have to do the same thing. We must trust God more because growing up is sometimes painful.

The first step of Naomi's growth was understanding that she needed to return to the God she knew to be the only God. This must have been agonizing for both women. For Naomi, going home with nothing but the clothes on her back must have been a torturous thought. What would the people say abut her? Burdened with the thought of what people might say, Naomi had also believed that God had been bitter toward her, so bitter that He had not blessed her. Such testimonies of discouragement are common among the immature.

On the other hand, Ruth's first step of growth was to trust that Naomi and her God were better than going back to her past—men- tally or physically. She did not know how Naomi's people would receive her, nor did she have a clue about how two single women would survive in a society where women needed men to take care of them. This must have been a great challenge for Ruth. But, she was determined to follow Naomi even though neither one believed that they would do more than just find food and shelter. They didn't know what to expect, but once they began to obey the God-established rules that were in place for them to follow, they begin to grow. As they stepped out further and further into a place where neither one had been before, God met them at every juncture. They kept growing and growing with no concern about what people would say about their methods of survival or operation. Because Naomi followed the divine plan of God for her people and Ruth followed Naomi unconditionally, they both received much more than they expected. They trusted God regardless of what the situation looked like. In fact, Naomi told Ruth before they left that she could not help her get a husband, which was key to young women in those days. But as Naomi matured, she began to realize and understand that God had something in place to help her get a husband for Ruth.

The Young Timothy

Marking his own place in the annals of spiritual maturity is Timothy. Timothy was a young man, chronologically, compared to his spiritual age. When Paul first met Timothy, he was young in Christ; in fact, he may have even been a new Christian, but he certainly was not mature. The apostle Paul noticed him on his second missionary journey and chose the young Timothy to travel with him. Paul began Timothy's maturation process by physically and spiritually circumcising (removing the unneeded parts) him. Although Paul could have chosen anybody to leave in charge, Timothy had matured to the point of being trusted to feed and lead people much older than he was in the natural.

Just as Ruth followed Naomi, Timothy followed and traveled with Paul and learned from him—so much so that he played a major role in the remainder of Paul's second missionary journey. In Acts chapter 17 when the Apostle Paul was forced to leave because of trouble brought on by the Jews of Thessalonica, he left Timothy with Silas in Macedonia. Their assignment was to strengthen the work in Macedonia. Timothy must have known the challenge of staying behind, but he remained and grew during this process. Later, in Acts 18, Silas and Timothy rejoined Paul in Athens. Timothy was in training with Paul or Silas for a period of time, but as he grew spiritually he was able to take on more responsibility. As a result, Paul later sent Timothy back to Thessalonica alone. He was able to send him unac- companied because Timothy had grown so much spiritually that he was able to do the job by himself. His assignment was to establish and to encourage the Thessalonians in the faith. Timothy did an excellent job of doing just that. He reported back to Paul the results of his work in 1 Thessalonians 3:6:

> *"But Timothy has just now come to us from you and has brought good news about your faith and love. He has told us that you always have pleasant memories of us and that you long to see us, just as we also long to see you." (NIV)*

Timothy must have been a part of Paul's trials and tribulations, but he did not quit or turn back. He continued to mature and grow up in the things of God and in the knowledge of Jesus Christ being taught by Paul and Silas. Timothy's report of the faith and love of the Thessalonians greatly encouraged Paul; but Paul must have been more encouraged by Timothy's spiritual development.

Timothy went with Paul on his third missionary journey. According to Acts 19:22, it was during this trip that Paul sent his helpers, Timothy and Erastus, to Macedonia while he stayed in the province of Asia a little longer. Notice that on this particular assignment Timothy had the lead position. He'd matured to a position of trust that was a more difficult assignment. Timothy was one of the people who accompanied Paul along the coast of Asia Minor on his way to Jerusalem, and he was with Paul for a time when he was imprisoned in Rome. All of this must have been a great learning and maturing process for Timothy! The Apostle Paul was confronted with major oppositions wherever he went once he himself had reached a level of spiritual maturity. And Timothy? Well, his spiritual development continued until, finally, we see him as having been the first bishop of Ephesus according to *Nelson's Illustrated Bible Dictionary*.

Personally, I ask God from time to time to give me grace to love and trust Him more. The more one grows, the more one loves and trusts the Lord.

Chapter 8
Commanded to Mature

Jesus taught His disciples by His own life example how they were to grow up in the things of God. When Jesus walked the earth, all that the people of God had as a pattern by which to live godly lives was the Torah or the Pentateuch (which means instructions or the law of Moses). Jesus gave them another instruction of what God wanted in the New Testament. He did this by teaching them what the *Word In Life Study Bible* calls the "Christian Torah." The Christian Torah contains sermons in the book of Matthew that explain the day-to-day application of the truth of the teachings of Christ. These Sermons contained teachings that were totally different from what Jesus' disciples had been taught in the past. Jesus took the time in each sermon to teach about moral and ethical behaviors. He taught about the kingdom of God, and what is expected of those who belong to the family of God. But, it was Jesus' Sermon on the Mount that taught them how to be mature and how to grow up.

In Matthew 5:48 we are encouraged to "Be ye therefore perfect, even as your Father which is in heaven is perfect." In this context, the word for "perfect" is the Greek work "teleios" (tel'-i-os), *which means in various applications of labor, growth, mental and moral character, etc.—of full age and completeness*. Also in this chapter, we can find Jesus talking to the rich young man and telling him, "If thou wilt be perfect, go and sell that thou hast, and give to the poor, and thou shalt have treasure in heaven: and come and follow me" (Matthew

19:21). We know when we read the rest of the passage that the rich young man did not give up all of his earthly wealth to grow up in Christ and follow Him. The same is true of some of us today. We do not want to sell out to Christ and be willing to trust God for everything. Doing so would take complete trust in God and complete surrender to the leading and teaching of the Holy Spirit that comes only with spiritual maturity.

Jesus' disciples learned to grow up in the things of God through this kind of teaching. It must have been difficult for them to learn the Beatitudes, which teaches that the way God wants us to operate is completely different from our points of view or even our points of reference. In our day and time, it is hard for us to let go of "an eye for an eye" and embrace our enemies with love. Yet, if we ever want to be spiritually mature, we must come to a place where we refrain from retaliation and learn to love our enemies.

Jesus taught His disciples to be salt and light. They were no longer to focus on themselves and their families' spiritual well being only, but they now had to look out for others. Jesus wanted His followers to influence the world both spiritually and morally.

Jesus further taught His disciples spiritual disciplines, treasures on the earth, judging right and wrong, asking and receiving and obedience. Jesus' bottom line in teaching His disciples was to BE LIKE ME. In order to be like Jesus, they had to grow up in the things of God and commit themselves to obey the words of God that He was speaking and teaching. Being like Jesus also meant that they had to die to themselves and follow Him. He taught the disciples that they must be able to go through what He went through, do what He did, serve others, and proclaim the message of Christ.

Jesus taught these powerful principles through the following five major speeches (the Christian Torah):

The Sermon on the Mount (Matthew 5:1-7:27)

In this sermon, Jesus talks about the kingdom being at hand and about the lifestyle of the kingdom. Jesus is the King, and in this sermon He talks about how we should live and the rules associated with the kingdom. *This is an explanation of what Jesus wanted His followers to be and to do. In other words, this oration answers the question, "How should Christians conduct themselves in their relationship to God, to fellow believers and to other people?"* It contains information that sets the standard for Christian character and influence. The moral laws of God are clearly stated in this sermon. These moral laws include, but are not limited to, the Christian's prayer, the ambitions of Christians, and the relationships that Christians have with their brothers, their Father, and others. Proper Christian conduct is paramount in God's kingdom.

Instructions to His Chosen Twelve (Matthew 9:35–10:42)

Jesus selected twelve of His disciples, appointed them as apostles, and prepared them to do the work of His ministry. The work of His ministry included giving them the authority to drive out evil spirits and to heal every disease. This is the sermon Jesus used to give them instructions on how to conduct themselves when they were sent out to minister.

Parables of the Kingdom Given to His Disciples (Matthew 13:1-52)

Every king has an operational plan for his kingdom. Jesus is no exception. Jesus is King of kings and Lord of lords; He has a plan of operation for His kingdom. These parables serve as a manual of operation with a specific plan for each principle's success. Every subject of the kingdom is expected to follow the plan if they expect to enjoy the bene- fits of the kingdom. However, those who are not a part of the kingdom should not expect kingdom benefits. For that reason, Jesus used parables to give a plain and general explanation of kingdom principles. This sermon uses these parables to explain the operation of the kingdom.

Instructions on Community Given to the Disciples (Matthew 18:1-35)

Jesus gave instructions on the spiritual and social conduct of Christians in regards to other people and the community at large.

The Olivet Discourse Given to His Disciples (Matthew 24:1-25-46)

This sermon discusses the end time events and the triumphant return of Christ.

The directions, principles, rules, and commands in these scriptures are what determine levels of maturity in many cases. Jesus explains what to do, how to act, how to respond, how to get along with people and how to conduct business God's way, but many Christians say to God, " I love you, but I will not follow your rules." These are usually babies, but not all of the time. Even those at a more mature level will neglect to follow God's rules. The more we can say "yes" and do what is asked in these scriptures, the more mature we have grown. Remember, Jesus said "If you love Me, obey Me..." From these teachings of Jesus, it is evident that we are commanded to grow up and mature in the things of God.

As we endeavor to be like Jesus Christ we must grow. This is a daily and a constant process. We will not be able to complete it here on earth, but as the scripture says in I John 3:2, " Beloved, now are we the sons of God, and it doth not yet appear what we shall be: but we know that, when he shall appear, we shall be like him; for we shall see him as he is." Each day we grow closer to Him, desiring to be more like Him.

Biblical Terms and Explanations

Salvation

Salvation is defined as deliverance from the power of sin; redemption. In the Old Testament, the word salvation sometimes refers to deliverance from enemies, danger of captivity, slavery, or sickness, etc. But salvation finds its deepest meaning in the spiritual realm of life. Man's universal need for salvation is one of the clearest teachings of the Bible.

The need for salvation goes back to man's fall from a position of living eternally with God to a life of spiritual and physical death. The definition of death is a change of place or conditions. The fall of man and his removal from the Garden of Eden (Genesis 3) caused him to live a limited physical life marked by strife and difficulty. Increasingly, corruption and violence dominated his world (Genesis 6:11-13). This is true today, perhaps even more so than when it first happened.

God is big on salvation. We notice in Genesis how He saved the earth from darkness, how He saved Adam and Eve from their sin and also how He used Noah to save mankind after the flood. The salvation of Noah and his family was viewed by the Apostle Peter as a pattern of that full salvation we receive in Christ (1 Peter 3:18-22). God also saved Lot from the destruction that fell upon Sodom and Gomorrah, and He saved the children of Israel from the tyranny of slavery in Egypt. Aren't you and I grateful that God is big on salvation?

This doctrine of salvation reached its fulfillment in the death of Christ on our behalf. Jesus' mission was to save the world from sin and the wrath of God (Matthew 1:21; John 12:47; Romans 5:9). During His earthly ministry, salvation was brought to us by His presence and the power of faith (Luke 19:9-10). Now, our salvation is based on His death and resurrection (Mark 10:25).

The salvation that comes through Christ may be described in three tenses: past, present, and future. When a person believes in Christ, he is saved (Acts 16:31). We are saved from every sin past, present and future.

Those things in our past that the enemy likes to remind us of are forgiven and there is no penalty to pay. The penalty has been paid by Jesus Christ, and those past sins of thought, word, or deed have no hold over us because we are free from the penalty. We as believers are free from our past, and we can boast just as Paul did when he said that he had done no man wrong. He had an understanding that God does not even remember the things that he did or the sins he committed in his past.

We are also in the process of being saved from the power of sin (Romans 8:13; Philippians 2:12). Presently, sin has no power over us because we are free from the power of sin; therefore, we can live and enjoy a victorious life! I did not say a "trouble-free life" because being saved means that we are targets of the enemy—but we have power over our enemies' tactics. Simply stated, this actually means that we can live an abundant life here on earth if we grow up in the things of God. In John 10:10b, Jesus said, "I am come that they might have life, and that they might have it more abundantly." Life is what God gave us through Adam in the beginning. In physical terms, life is the time between birth and death. Because God is the source of life, it is a gift from Him. He first filled Adam with the breath of life in the second chapter of the book of Genesis. But when Adam and Eve fell, the period of their birth and death was defined as life. But we know that originally, God defined life as eternity with Him—being the source of all life. God wants us to live our lives as Christians with Him now, and He wants the life that we live to be an abundant life.

Many Christians are waiting to see Jesus in heaven to get the abundant life. Many others are waiting for His return to get the abundant life. But as sons, He offers the abundant life to us now.

As sons of God we have the authority that Jesus Christ had; how- ever, we will not be granted that authority as long as we are too young to handle the job. Jesus was able to handle the storms of life without falling apart. We can do what he did and more (John 14:12). He wants to give us the fullness of Himself, for His glory, while we remain on this earth.

Herman Riffel writes, "I am impressed that the aim of the New Testament teaching is to bring God's children into maturity; a maturity that includes a person's full acceptance and love of himself, of all other, and of God. Maturity is not an impossible goal for the future but a developing process of the body, soul and spirit, so that at each level the person can appropriate responsibility for life in all three realms, and can enter into maturity. The church has spent much of its efforts in bringing children into the family of God. It is evident that as a child must be born to enter the world, so must a person be born of the Spirit to enter the Kingdom of God. Jesus said, "In truth, in very truth I tell you unless a man has been born over again he cannot see the Kingdom of God." (John 3:3 NEB). But Jesus never stopped there in His teaching. When the man who had been wild was told to go home alone so that growth could begin (Mark 5:1-20), He wanted to stay with Jesus, as a little child prefers to stay with his mother, but Jesus immediately started him off to maturity.[8]"

Finally, we shall be saved from the very presence of sin (Romans 13:11; Titus 2:12-13). God releases into our lives today the power of Christ's resurrection (Romans 6:4) and allows us a foretaste of our future lives as His children (2 Corinthians 1:22; Ephesians 1:14). Our experience of salvation will be complete when Christ returns (Hebrews 9:28) and the kingdom of God is fully revealed (Matthew 13:41-43).

Sanctification

Sanctification is the process of God's grace by which the believer is separated from sin and becomes dedicated to God's righteousness. Accomplished by the Word of God (John 17:7) and the Holy Spirit (Romans 8:3-4), sanctification results in holiness, or purification from the guilt and power of sin. This is the process used by the Lord to bring God's children from infancy to adulthood. Growing up in the things of God can be fun, but it can also be painful. Learning to obey the Lord is one of the primary things that we must do. It is impossible to grow to be like Jesus if we do not obey the Word of God. Obedience is accomplished by suffering. Suffering is the way that Jesus learned obedience, and it is also the way by which we must learn it. We know this to be true when we read from Hebrews 5:8: "Though he were a Son, yet learned he obedience by the things which he suffered." The Word of God makes it very apparent that it will be necessary for us to suffer in order to learn obedience and subsequently, to mature.

Justification

The process by which sinful human beings are made acceptable to a holy God is called "justification" or "justification by grace." Christianity is unique because of its teaching of justification by grace, which can be found in the third chapter of Romans. Simply stated, justification is God's declaration that the demands of His Law have been fulfilled in the righteousness of His Son. The basis for this justification is the death of Christ. Paul tells us that "God was in Christ reconciling the world to Himself, not imputing their trespasses to them" (2 Corinthians 5:19). This reconciliation covers all sin, "For by one offering He has perfected forever those who are being sanctified" (Hebrews 10:14). Justification, then, is based upon the work of Christ, accomplished through His blood (Romans 5:9) and brought to His people through His resurrection (Romans 4:25). There is nothing that we need to do in order to be justified except believe that Jesus is Savior and Lord and that He is the author and finisher of our faith. This helps us to understand that we can do nothing without Jesus Christ. We would be lost if we tried to justify ourselves to the Father. Because of this fact, we should always be in a position of giving God all of the honor, the glory and the praise for our position of good standing with the Father, Son and Holy Spirit.

Adoption
In the New Testament, the Greek word translated "adoption" literally means "placing as a son." It is important to note that the word "son" has no gender. Therefore, all who are adopted become sons. Adoption in the New Testament is a legal term that expresses the process by which a man brings another person into his family, endow- ing him with the status and privileges of a biological son or daughter. Christian adoption involves reconciliation—not only has God for- given us, but we also have been reconciled to him. We no longer carry enmity toward Him. God has shown His love for us by taking the initiative in restoring the fellowship that was damaged by our sin. As Paul puts it, "But God shows His love for us in that while we were ye sinners Christ died for us ...If while we were enemies we were reconciled, shall we be saved by his life" (Romans 5:8, 10). In adoption both sides are reconciled to one another.

Adoption also provides liberty for the children of God. The child of God is not a slave who obeys out of a sense of bondage or compulsion. Slaves live in fear of consequences should they fail to carry out their obligations, but Paul points out that as God's children, we need not fear the consequences of failing to live up to the law: "For all who are led by the Spirit of God are sons of God. For you did not receive the spirit of slavery to fall back into fear; but you have received the spirit of sonship. When we cry 'Abba! Father!' it is the Spirit Himself bearing witness with our spirit that we are children of God" (Romans 8:14-16). [9]

In the Old Testament, adoption was never common among the Israelites but was practiced by foreigners or by Jews who were influenced by foreign customs. Pharaoh's daughter adopted Moses (Exodus 2:10) and another pharaoh adopted Genubath, his wife's sister's son who was brought up in the royal palace and lived with Pharaoh's own children (1 Kings 11:20). Furthermore, there is no Hebrew word to describe the process of adoption. When the Pharaoh's daughter adopted Moses, the text says, "...he became her son." Since Moses was a type of Christ, we can see the foreshadowing of our adoption as sons of God in the New Testament. Adoption makes Christians heirs to all that the Father has for His sons, but as long as they remain children they are no different from servants or slaves and will have to remain in school. They cannot be released to do the work of an heir because they are still in bondage to the world: "Now I say, That the heir, as long as he is a child, differeth nothing from a servant, though he be lord of all; But is under tutors and governors until the time appointed of the father. Even so we, when we were children, were in bondage under the elements of the world" (Galatians 4:1-3). As Christians, we enjoy freedom in Christ, but if we do not grow up in Christ, we will continue to remain in bondage to the things of the enemy such as the spirit of offense, unforgiveness, hatred and the like. If we cannot overcome these things, how can we help anyone else?

Redemption

Redemption, defined in the Greek as apolutrosis, a "loosing" away; or lutrosis, a "loosing," particularly by paying a price; for other terms, is a comprehensive term employed in theology with reference to the special intervention of God for the salvation of mankind. Its meaning centers in the atoning work of Christ as the price paid for human redemption, and on account of which Christ is called the Redeemer. But along with this are other conceptions relating to the necessity for redemption, and also the various stages and measures in the redemptive economy and the effects of God's gracious work.

Christ is man's Redeemer; but as such, He is divinely appointed. The redemption He wrought manifests not only the love of the Son, but also that of the Father. The Holy Spirit, as well, is active in the administration of redemption. He preserves what Christ redeemed. The Trinity is a redemptive Trinity (see Romans 5:8; John 3:16; Matthew 28:19). Still, for the reason named above, the Son of God is the sole Redeemer of mankind. The word redemption implies antecedent bondage. Thus, the term refers primarily to man's subjection to the dominion and curse of sin (see Galatians 3:13; 1 Corinthians 15:56) and in a secondary sense, to the bondage of Satan as the head of the kingdom of darkness, and to the bondage of death as the penalty of sin (see Acts 26:18; Hebrews 2:14-15). Redemption from this bondage is represented in the scriptures as both universal and limited. It is universal in the sense that its advantages are freely offered to all. It is limited in the sense that it is effectual only with respect to those who meet the conditions of salvation announced in the gospel. For such, it is effectual in that persons receive forgiveness of sins and the power to lead a new and holy life. Satan is no longer their captor, and death has lost its sting and terror. Christians actually look forward to the redemption of the body (see Hebrews 2:9; Acts 3:19; Ephesians 1:7; Acts 26:18; 2 Timothy 2:26; 1 Corinthians 15:55-57; Romans 8:15-23).

Sons of God

Jesus Christ—The SON OF GOD

According to the *International Standard Bible Encyclopedia*, the use of this title in the Synoptics is explained as follows:

While the title "the Son of man" is always, except once, applied by Jesus to Himself, "the Son of God" is never applied by Jesus to Himself in the Synoptics. When, however, it is applied to Him by others, He accepts it in such a way as to assert His claim to it. Now and then He Himself employs the abbreviated form, "the Son," with the same intention; and He often speaks of God as "the Father" or "my Father" or "my Father who is in heaven in such a manner as to betray the consciousness that He is the Son of God."[10]

The encyclopedia goes on to say that the meaning in the Old Testament of "the Son of man" is a title designating the human side of our Lord's person. The title "the Son of God" seems as obviously to indicate the divine side. Yet in the Old Testament, being a foreshadow- ing of what was to come in the New Testament that Jesus Christ is the "Son of God," there were many expressions, in persons, that were used as types of Christ. The encyclopedia also gives a physical reason for Jesus being called the "Son of God." In this reference it goes on to say that by examining the use of the name "The Son of God" in the New Testament as applied by others to Jesus, the facts are far from simple, and it is not applied in a uniform sense. In Luke 1:35, the following reason for its use is given, "The Holy Spirit shall come upon thee, and the power of the Most High shall overshadow thee: wherefore also the holy thing which is begotten shall be called the Son of God." It is rather curious that this point of view does not seem to be adopted elsewhere, unless it is in the exclamation of the centurion at the foot of the cross when he declared, "Truly this was the Son of God" (Matthew 27:54).

In addition, the account of Father God calling Jesus His son in Matthew 3:17, "This is my beloved Son, in whom I am well pleased," is a clear indication that the Father wanted it known that Jesus was his Son. These words may also have been used to designate Jesus as the Messiah; but, found in the adjective "beloved," and the words "in whom I am well pleased," there is something personal, something beyond merely official recognition. After the Father announced this at Jesus' baptism, He later repeated it at the Scene of the Transfiguration.

Now every person who was listening to the Father knows that Jesus is His son. John the Baptist as well as all of those who were present at the baptism and the transfiguration were witnesses of God's divine proclamation. That group of hearers also included Satan. He also heard what the Father said about Jesus and he, too, called Jesus the "Son of God." This is confirmed by the words that were said to Jesus when Satan approached Him in the Temptation in the Wilderness: "If thou art the Son of God..." tempted Satan (Matthew 4:3). After this, even the demons acknowledged Jesus as the "Son of God." We see an example of this in Luke 4:41: "And devils also came out of many, crying out, and saying, Thou art Christ the Son of God. And he rebuking them suffered them not to speak: for they knew that he was Christ."

As the Son of God, Jesus came to fulfill prophecy and to do the work that was designated for the Son to accomplish. Jesus did what was given Him to do and now believers are commanded by Jesus Christ to carry on that same work as sons of God.

Spiritual Sonship
This term, as used in a theological sense, commonly denotes that act of God by which He restores penitent and believing men to their privileges as members of the divine family and makes them heirs of heaven. This act restores believers to the position that Adam and Eve had before the fall. Through Christ we are innocent of all of our sin and can come boldly before the throne of God as sons.

The Duty of Sons
The duty of sons of God is to be imitators of God. As beloved children we are to imitate the acts of our heavenly Father (Ephesians 5:1 NAS). This means that we must allow the spiritual growth that the Lord has made available to us to take its proper course.

Believers
The International Standard Bible Encyclopedia also

makes us aware of several different accounts of God calling people His sons. We know from Exodus 4:22, Yahweh, speaking of the Hebrew nation, said to Pharaoh, "Israel is my son, my first-born." Israel was referred to as a son because it was the object of Yahweh's special love and gracious choice. The term was also applied to the kings of Israel as representatives of the chosen nation. For example, in 2 Samuel 7:14, Yahweh says of Solomon, "I will be his father, and he shall be my son." Likewise, in Psalms 2:7, the coronation of a king is announced in an oracle from heaven announcing, "Thou art my son; this day have I begotten thee." Finally, in the New Testament, the title is applied to all saints, as in John 1:12, "But as many as received him, to them gave he the right to become children of God, even to them that believe on his name." When the title has such a range of application, it is obvious that the divinity of Christ cannot be inferred from the mere fact that it is applied to Him.

Since God our Father provided these examples in the Old Testament, which is the foreshadowing of the New Testament, it is natural to assume that its use in application to Jesus and the believers is manifested in the New Testament. Therefore, believers have a responsibility to live as sons of God, to do the work required of sons, and to accomplish all that is required of the body of Christ.

Spiritual Growth
The idea of spiritual growth is to enlarge or to increase spiritual level, or to grow up in the things of God.

Transformation of the Mind
The change of the moral character for the better (Romans

12:2) through the renewal of the thinking power is considered a transformation of the mind. Apostle Paul speaks of Christians being "transformed into the same image from glory to glory" in his second letter to the Corinthians. In the third chapter of this same letter, the gospel is spoken of as a mirror in which the glory of Christ gives itself to be seen. The Christian becomes so transformed by the Word of God that the same image, which he sees in the "mirror," which is the image of the glory of Christ, presents itself on him. When this happens, the Christian becomes like the image he sees—like the glorified Christ.

Milk as Spiritual Food
A believer that is unskillful in the word of righteousness is a baby who needs to feed on the basics or what we commonly call in the body of Christ—milk. A believer who consumes spiritual food as milk is not able to discern good from evil.

Meat as Spiritual Food
A believer that is older in spiritual development and is able to reason by use of his senses (which have been exercised) is said to feed upon meat or "strong meat." As a result, he or she is able to discern both good and evil.

Spiritual Maturity
A spiritually mature person is a believer who has become an elder in spiritual development. This term defines a spiritually mature believer, but not spiritual maturity itself.

The Will of God
The will of God can be expressed in three levels. The first level is the Sovereign Will of God—This is God's

purpose from eternity past to eternity future whereby He determines all that shall take place. The second level of the will of God is God's Moral Will. We have much of this—or at least what God wanted us to know of this—revealed to us in the Bible. The scripture tells us what God wants us to believe and how God wants us to behave. That is the moral will of God, and it is very clear. There is also a third level of God's will in which many people believe and it is called God's Individual Will. This is what we are usually concerned about when we ask, "How can I know God's will?" When it comes to God's individual will, we seem to believe that God has our lives mapped out on a blackboard in heaven which we must glimpse in order to make the choices God desires for us.

God works out His sovereign will through all men and women. He has revealed to us His moral will, but He doesn't necessarily reveal His specific, individual will to us. It's possible that He does this at special times for some Christians, but we have no solid biblical testimony on that point. Unfortunately, this hasn't stopped many Christians from putting God's individual will on the same biblical footing as God's sovereign and moral will.[11]

Chapter 9
The Timeline for Spiritual Maturity

When does it begin?
Spiritual Maturity begins at birth in the body of Christ. Once we become born-again believers in Christ Jesus, we begin the process of growing up.

When does it end?
The growth process never ends. We constantly grow, and we must choose to continue to grow. We can never completely grow up because we have too much to learn. I do not believe that we were created to get to a place of not needing to learn and grow. God is so awesome that we could study for eternity long and find that there is no end to the possibilities in Him.

What is the process?
As stated earlier, the process whereby we mature is sanctification. Sanctification is accomplished through the leading, teaching, and the power of the Holy Spirit. We cannot do anything without the Holy Spirit. It is a slow and sometimes agonizing process, but it is always rewarding.

How do we prepare to grow?
Preparation is accomplished through Christian education, prayer, fasting, the preached Word and the taught Word. We prepare ourselves by following principles from the areas just mentioned. According to Bill Bright, an American evangelist and founder of Campus Crusade for Christ, there are five principles of Christian growth that will help us prepare ourselves to grow up in the things of

God. In the words of Bill Bright:

"The first two principles that we must follow are: 1. We must study God's Word and 2. We must pray. This helps us deepen our relationship with God. This could be called our vertical relationship.

Through the Bible, God communicates to us; through prayer, we communicate with Him. The next two principles we must follow are: 3. Fellowship with other Christians and 4. Witness for Christ. These help us reach out to others. This could be called our horizontal relationship. In fellowship, we communicate with other Christians about our Savior and the bond He gives us with one another. In witnessing, we communicate with non-Christians. We tell them about Jesus, what He has done for us, and what He desires to do for them. Principle five, We must obey God, this is the core of the growth. As we obey Him, we experience increasing joy, peace and fellowship with the Lord Jesus Christ and fellow believers. We also become increasingly more mature in our Christian walk. If you follow these principles, you can be sure that you will grow toward spiritual maturity in Christ.[12]"

Are all Christians required to mature spiritually?

It is God's desire for all of His children to grow up and enjoy all the things that He has for us. The only way Christians can enjoy all that God has for them is to grow up. Maturity is necessary to be able to understand and handle certain things. It is a must. At one point Jesus had to say to those who followed Him that there were many things that He desired to say to them, but they were not able to bear them at that time. We find this in John 16:12-13: "I have much more to say to you, more than you can now bear. But when he, the Spirit of truth, comes, he will guide you into all truth. He will not speak on his own; he will speak only what he hears, and he will tell you what is yet to come (NIV)." Jesus was basically saying that those who were listening were not old enough to bear His words and they needed the Holy Spirit to help them grow in the truth and the knowledge of God.

Chapter 10
Spiritual Maturity, Psychological Age and Physiological Age

According to Robert Barron, J. Omar Brubaker and Robert E. Clark, authors of Understanding People, each individual advances through various stages in life. Each person advances through these stages distinctly and differently until they reach maturity. The same is true of spiritual development. These authors report the following three major divisions, or periods in life:

- Childhood (birth to 11 years)
- Adolescence (12-17)
- Adult (18 and up)

In spiritual maturity, the childhood years that are mentioned above correspond with the childhood years of spiritual maturity in that they are the years of dependence and preparation. Childhood years lay the foundation for the remainder of the years of development. They are the years that include vital preschool development (babies in Christ). This is a time of developing personality structures and forming lifelong habits. This is also the stage in spiritual development where good habits must be learned (young children in Christ). These routines include personal Bible study habits (learning the Word of God by read- ing daily) and prayer habits. This a time to begin to learn that prayer is necessary and must also be done daily. Prayerlessness is sin. Babies need to learn that early in their development.

The authors of *Understanding People* report that the adolescent stage in a person's life is spent in preparation and training for the transition to adulthood. Sometimes college and career years are included in this stage. Young people seek their independence during this period and begin to understand themselves as total persons. Great changes take place physically as they reach new intellectual heights. This group corresponds with the young men (Adolescents and Teenagers) level of spiritual maturity. They, like their counterparts, have flux in their emotions. They often doubt counsel from teachers or parents and want to make decisions for themselves. The authors further report that this period serves as a transition from childhood to adulthood. Adolescents begin to discover what contributions they can make. As they struggle to find themselves, they are often misunderstood, but with careful guidance and direction they can emerge with a well-balanced personality. The same is true of spiritual adolescents. With proper direction from pastors, teachers and mature Christians, they, too, can become well-balanced Christians as they continue the maturing process.

Barron, Brubaker, and Clark conclude their discussion on this subject with the adults. They write that various events are associated with becoming adults. Voting age, military service, college, career pursuits, marital status, and the amount of responsibility people assume all affect movement into adulthood. The same is true for the spiritual adults. They begin to take leadership positions in the body of Christ that may include anything from a mother or father, role mod- els for the young or formal leadership in the church such as deacons, elders, trustees and stewards. They may also head up other ministries in the church such as the Superintendent of Sunday school or Minister of Education. All of these require a greater level or responsibility and authority.

Although *psychological* and *social* development are similar to one another, they are not the same. They can be best be understood by examining the personality development of a person. Christians are confronted with two aspects of personality development. One aspect relates to the natural human personality and the other is the Christian personality. The authors of Understanding People have this to say about the human personality:

> "**Human Personality** -Personality, in the natural human sense, is a term describing the total of what people are physically, intellectually, socially, emotionally, and spiritually. It includes every aspect and area of life. From birth, personality is influenced and molded by many forces—Heredity and environment being the major forces. Within the environment, a person is influenced mainly by family, school, church, peer group, and society."[13]

We know that the human personality development will undergo a change when a person becomes a Christian. However, the change is based on a new birth and a renewing of the person's mind. Understanding People, when discussing Christian personality, puts it this way:

> "Christian education provides an additional perspective in the development of personality. The goal should be a wholesome and well-balanced personality which means spiritual balance as well as intellectual, emotional, social, and physical."

For a Christian personality there must be a definite conversion experience (John 3:3). The sinful nature with which people are born must be changed (Romans 3:23; 6:12; 6:23). Christ alone can give new life, for He died for sinful people upon the cross (Acts 4:12). Everyone who receives Christ as Savior is born again and is given new life (John 1:12; 3:3-6).

Even when natural human personality is well developed, new birth is necessary for a mature, well-balanced Christian personality (Ephesians 4:11-16). Christ provides for a person's spiritual development through the power of the indwelling Holy Spirit (Galatians 5:22-23). Parents and Christian leaders share by their example of personal experience and thus help others know the joy of an integrated Christian personality.[14]"

We notice, at least from this group of well-respected authors, that while it is necessary to experience a new birth to develop the Christian personality, we cannot disregard the natural order of human development altogether. We must take what we have and allow the Holy Spirit to spiritually develop our Christian personalities. This is something that becomes evident when we see a personality change of a new Christian or even an older one. We have to have a personality development in both situations. Therefore, we can safely state that the *psychological* and *physiological* age of a person does play a part in spiritual development, but the natural process is not the means for developing spiritual maturity. This can only be accomplished through the Holy Spirit.

There are many human growth and development theories in use today. Each of the theorists uses developmental stages to present their theories. The authors of *Understanding People* have included most of the significant ones in their book on the subject. Some of them are as follows:

Intellectual Stages

Jean Piaget, a noted developmental psychologist, describes four stages in intellectual development through childhood and adolescence that are distinct and qualitatively different from birth to about two years, a period during which children learn through experiences using their senses and self-discovery through activity; from about two to seven years, during which children judge things by their appearance and begin to use symbols through language they are acquiring; from about seven to eleven years, during which children are more logical, and learn to classify and put items in sequence and to communicate through concrete thinking; and from about twelve years through adulthood, during which thinking becomes more theoretical and abstract.

Psychosocial Stages

Erik Erikson, a developmental psychologist and psychoanalyst who is widely known for his psychosocial research, described eight stages of development that encompass all ages of human life. He views personality formation as a continuing process throughout childhood, adolescence, and adulthood. Four of his stages relate to children through eleven years of age. These stages are: Trust vs. Mistrust (birth to one year), Autonomy vs. Shame and Doubt (two to three years), Initiative vs. Guilt (four to five years), and Industry vs. Inferiority (six to eleven years).

In adolescence and adulthood, he suggests four stages: Ego Identity vs. Role Confusion, Intimacy vs. Isolation, Generatively vs. Stagnation, and Integrity vs. Despair. Erikson indicates that individuals must make major adjustments to their social environment and self in each stage of life.

Moral Development Stages

Famous for his Theory of Moral Development, psychologist Lawrence Kohlberg identifies six well-defined stages at three different levels through childhood and adolescence based on a sense of right and wrong. These stages represent growth of moral concepts or ways of judging, and not moral behavior. His stages are based on Piaget's stages of Cognitive Development, which are the Pre-Conventional Level (based on punishments and rewards), the Conventional Level (based on social conformity), and the Post-Conventional Level (based on moral principles). As individuals develop in their thinking processes, they can make moral judgments, and they exhibit examples of kinds of behavior that are typical at each level identified.

Each of these theories includes completion of developmental tasks as a means of determining progress. In addition, each has well-defined stages of developmental growth. During each stage, individuals should make certain progress and adjustments that are typical of that particular stage in life while keeping in mind that each stage must be completed successfully. Failure to progress according to the normal age group pattern will lead to unhappiness in the individual, disapproval by the society, and difficulty with later tasks.

Among the developmental tasks, four- to five-year-old children learn to dress themselves, six- to eight-year-old children learn to read and write, adolescents develop realistic concepts of themselves, and young adults often select life partners or choose careers. Completing these tasks at each level indicates the degrees of maturity persons have reached.

The same is true of spiritual development. Failure to progress according to the normal age group pattern will lead to unhappiness in the individual, disapproval by church leadership to accomplish cer- tain tasks, stunted spiritual growth, difficulty with later spiritual tasks and failure to live the spiritual abundant Christian life that Jesus Christ intended Christians to live.

While all of these human developmental theories serve their purpose, the one most closely related to Christian spiritual growth is Eric Erikson's Psychosocial Stages. I use Erikson's Psychosocial Stages to compare natural human growth with Christian spiritual growth. Erikson uses stages of growth, but I use spiritual levels of growth for my spiritual growth and developmental chart that you will view a little later.

Since we have discussed both psychology and physiology as they relate to spiritual maturity, we must ask ourselves, "Does this authority follow the authority received during the natural process of human psychosocial stages?" and "What spiritual authority comes with each stage of spiritual maturity?"

Understanding the authority that comes with natural development helps us to grasp the complexity of spiritual development. During the natural course of a person's life from birth to adulthood, people pass through stages of development. Individual stages have similar characteristics and can be grouped into common areas. The same can be said for Christian spiritual maturity.

Growing up in the natural and in the spiritual is inevitable, but where you are in the process is sometimes a mystery. If you get stuck at any stage, you are going to find it impossible to function as an adult. You cannot function as an adult unless you mature to the adult level. When we examine the upcoming chart, we find some interest- ing observations, similarities and differences between this chart and the spiritual chart that follows. Please notice that Erikson's chart is based upon growing older and acting older naturally. The older you get the more mature you are expected to become.

My (White's) spiritual chart, on the other hand, is based upon growing older spiritually—but being younger as it concerns receiving and obeying the leading of the Holy Spirit.

Notice, also, that the first four stages on Erikson's chart match the baby level on White's chart. Babies totally trust their parents and are absolutely confident that their parents will not allow anything bad to happen to them. I have seen parents throw a baby across the room to the other parent and the baby was laughing all the way. It never occurred to the baby that he might fall to the floor and hurt himself. But, we mustn't remain as spiritual babies.

We can see from these first four stages of Erikson's chart that many developmental activities need to be completed before a person continues to grow. This observation correlates with White's chart, especially in the Emphasis column. The other four stages are similar in structure but different in function:

Erikson's Psychosocial Stages Chart[15]

Stage	Age	Emphasis	Success	Failure
1 Trust vs Mistrust	1st year Oral Sensory	Satisfying basic physical and emotional needs	1. Sense of drive, purpose, trust in others 2. Trustworthiness as far as self is concerned	1. Chronic 2. Suspiciousness 3. Sense of doom 4. Compensatory over optimism
2 Autonomy vs. Shame/doubt	1-3 years Muscular-Anal	Exploration and developing self-reliance	1. Self control 2. Willpower	1. Feelings of shame and doubt possible future perversions
3 Initiative vs. Guilt	4-5 Locomotor Genital	Achieving a sense of competence and initiative	1. Direction/Purpose 2. The ability to glory in changes 3. The formation of moral sense	1. Guilt and inhibitions 2. Restriction of curiosity
4 Industry vs. Inferiority	6-12 years Latency	Setting and attaining personal goals	1. Method and Competency	1. Lack of organization 2. Feelings of inferiority
5 Identity vs Role confusion	12-18 years Puberty & Adolescence	Testing limits, achieving a self-identity	1. Capacity for fidelity and devotion	1. Shifted, confused or fragmented identity
6 Intimacy vs Isolation	18-35 years Young Adult	Achieving intimate interpersonal relationships	1. Affiliation and love	1. Isolation
7 Generativity vs Stagnation	35-65 years Adulthood	Helping next generation, being productive	1. Generativity 2. Production 3. Care	1. No generativity 2. No production 3. No care
8 Integrity vs Despair	65+ years Maturity	Integration of life activities, feeling worthwhile	1. Wisdom 2. Look at life as necessary and adequate	1. Despair, inability to let go of youthful dreams

UNDERSTANDING SPIRITUAL MATURITY

Dr. White's Spiritual Levels Chart

Spiritual Level	Spiritual Age	Spiritual Emphasis	Spiritual Success	Spiritual Failure
1 Babies 0-32 Points	0-1 years * Self is alive—Functions as a mature adult in the natural * Learning to let go of self and to trust God	* Satisfying basic spiritual needs * Feeds on milk * Focused on themselves * Exercises their faith for their own benefit	* Trusts church leadership * Trusts themselves * Trusts their salvation	* Lacks knowledge of good and evil * Unskillful in the word * Major struggles with the flesh
2 Young Children 33-64 Points	1-2 years * Self less alive—Functions as a young adult in the natural * Learning to submit to the leading of the Holy Spirit	* Makes spiritual choices * Attentive to personal and public Bible study * Exercises their faith for their own benefit	* Ability to set goals to overcome some of the struggles of the flesh * Forming good Bible study habits	* Lacks understanding of the Bible knowledge that they have received * Easy prey for deception
3 Young Men (Adolescents and Teenagers) 65-96 Points	2-4 years * Dying to self in a great measure—Functions as an adolescent or teenager in the natural *Transitioning trust from self to God	* Begins to practice biblical principles * Exercises their faith for Christ and then for themselves	* Strong in character * Devotion to Christ * Devotion to family, personal matters and church	* Struggles with self identity in Christ * Struggles with submission to authority * Struggles with transition to the next level
4 Young Adults 97-128 Points	4-10 years * Self almost completely dead —Functions as a young child in the natural * Trust the leading of the Holy Spirit more than self	* Puts more trust in God than in people * Exercises their faith for Christ and for the benefit of others * Actively seeking God's will for their lives	* Operates as a servant of the Lord * Flees from youth lust * The Word of God abides in them	* Struggles with speaking the truth in love * Struggles with more frequent spiritual battles
5 Mature Adults (Fathers) 129-160 Points	10-20 years * Self completely dead —Functions as a baby in the natural * Does not trust self at all— Follows the leading of the Holy Spirit most of the time	* Exercises faith for Christ and for the benefit of others * Counts all worldly accomplishments as loss * Rarely focuses on self-led by the Holy Spirit * Integrity	* Walks in love on all occasions * Has an intimate relationship with Christ * Reproduces themselves often *Walks in the power of His resurrection * The will of God is paramount	* Zealousness for church work may cause compromise of intimate time with Christ * Struggles with wanting more for their sons than they want for themselves

These two charts give us an idea of what amount/kind of authority each stage or level enjoys. We can surmise from the emphasis and success columns that the level of authority increases at each stage or level. As a child grows in the natural, more authority is manifested in their lives. For instance, no one expects a one-month old infant to walk; but a one-month old infant is expected to feel, hear and cry. So, that becomes the level of authority that they enjoy. The walking will not normally occur before they reach 7 months old or older. Until that time they will not receive the authority to walk from their parents. Once they learn to walk they will receive the authority to walk, but they will not be allowed to walk until that time. We know from observing babies that they always want to get down from the arms that are holding them to walk, crawl or move into places where they have not yet matured enough to enter.

Likewise, children must reach a level of proficiency in the first three stages of Erikson's Psychosocial Chart before they will be allowed to go to public school. They must be able to walk, talk, have self control (bathroom skills), follow directions, have proper motor skills, etc. in order to be trusted to accomplish the activities necessary to function in school. If they cannot meet these requirements, they will not be granted the authority to go into the normal school pro- gram. Instead, they will need to participate in a special education program, designed especially for them, that will assist them in preparing for the proper school curriculum.

The same is true for the children of God. They must show that they have reached a certain level of spiritual maturity before they will receive the authority from church leaders (pastors, elders, etc.) or God to accomplish certain tasks. For instance, a pastor will not normally assign a baby in Christ to a key leadership position in the church. White's chart on Spiritual Levels of Growth gives a clear indication that the emphasis and the success level of babies does not lend itself to leadership positions. They are looking to be led by church leadership, not to be church leaders. Pastors will not assign or recommend them for leadership until they grow more because such an assignment is sure to bring disaster to the auxiliary involved or perhaps the government of the church.

Notice from White's chart that as a person grows spiritually, he or she attains more spiritual authority. The more authority that a Christian has, the more they can accomplish in the kingdom of God. For instance, one would not expect a young child, (spiritual age one to two years) to lead an intercessory prayer group. Intercessors need to have a desire for God to move in the situations of others. They also need to have the faith that God will answer their prayers on behalf of other people and situations. Because they have not yet matured to a level of being able to have faith for more than themselves, spiritual babies should never be placed in these types of leadership positions.

The same is true in the natural. Glancing at Erikson's chart, we know not to expect a six-year-old child to marry because they are not psychologically ready (no capacity for fidelity and devotion), nor are they physically ready (not yet developed the physical ability to reproduce) to be joined with someone in holy matrimony. For that reason, no one in their right mind would give a six-year-old the authority to get married. The same chart lets us know not to expect three-year-olds to drive the family car to the grocery store. They have not matured enough to receive the authority for this kind of activity.

We can conclude from these two charts that authority comes with natural and spiritual maturity.

Chapter 11
What Stunts Spiritual Growth?

Heredity and Environment

The book *Understanding People* reports two major factors that influence psychosocial personality development. They are heredity and environment. Both of these interact with each other in develop- ing unique personalities. Maturity results from these complex forces operating over an extended period of time. It is impossible to deter- mine exactly how much heredity or how much environment contributes since they cannot be understood apart from each other. Heredity gives an innate capacity and sets boundaries for potential development. Environment cultivates or hinders the development. The individual's emotional structure combines them into a unique personality. Heredity, of course, consists of the genes inherited from parents. For instance, the ability to learn is inherited, but knowledge is not. Likewise, children have little control over their environment. Their environment is controlled by their parents and those with whom they live. The most important environmental influences affecting children are family, school, church, peer groups, and society.

The family is the key environment for the most impressionable years. Children are influenced by the sentiments, opinions, and moral standards where they live. Imitation comes first and comprehension later. In the home children must find the love, understanding, and training they need.[16]

Ignorance of the Word of God

Similar issues inhibit spiritual growth. While heredity in the natural is needed for personality development, heredity in the spirit is needed for spiritual growth. Christians need the heredity that Jesus Christ offers them as heirs. Once Christians become members of the body of Christ, they become children of God and they are entitled to the rights of sons. Jesus commands us to be like Him, therefore we know that we have the genes in us that give us the ability to obey His command. That, of course, is the Holy Spirit. However, we need to study the Word of God (Bible) in order to get the knowledge we need to grow up in the things of God. Therefore, not studying the Word of God is going to hinder our spiritual growth. There is no substitute for Christian education in the spiritual growth process. Without it, Christians are ignorant of the Word of God. God does say that His people perish because of lack of knowledge.

The other factor that promotes or stunts spiritual growth is the environment. Just as in the natural, Christians have no control over their environment. God plants each one in the body of Christ at a local church where they can grow and bloom. The pastor of that particular congregation is the one that God uses to educate His people. The environmental influences that affect the spiritual growth of Christians are parents (pastors), school (Christian and secular education), peer groups, and the Christian society (others in the body of Christ).

Recognizing what causes stunted growth is just as important as realizing the penalties of the same. Refusing to grow has some serious consequences. These consequences are the results of the vulnerability of immaturity. God wants us to grow so that the cares of this world and the tricks of Satan will no longer cause havoc in our lives. Immaturity makes us an easy target for Satan. It is not a sin to be immature, but immaturity causes us to be pulled into sinful activity more often than not.

Once we start the process of spiritual maturity we will, at some point in our growth, become immune to certain things that will cause us to be pulled to and fro by winds, strange doctrines and life situations that feel good to our flesh. These things are promulgated and instigated by our enemy Satan. Three examples are offense, unforgiveness, and refusing to be merciful.

Offense

Offense is a snare of Satan. Many times we believe that we have a right to be offended because someone has taken something that belongs to us. It may be our time, talent, money, health or loved ones, but the Word of God says that we must resist evil. In fact, Jesus Himself tells us this thing. The book of Matthew recalls what Jesus had to say about this matter in 5:39-41: "But I say unto you, That ye resist not evil: but whosoever shall smite thee on thy right cheek, turn to him the other also. And if any man will sue thee at the law, and take away thy coat, let him have thy cloak also. And whosoever shall compel thee to go a mile, go with him twain." According to this principle and command we should never stay at a position of offense with any- one. Now some believe that this passage is not for the New Testament. But how can we go backwards? If this principle was practiced in the Old Testament, how much more should we practice it?

In the Old Testament under the LAW, an eye for eye was good. But even under the LAW we see this principle was practiced in the old Joseph, the son of Jacob. His brothers whom he loved tried to kill him, sold him into slavery and forgot about him. But Joseph never became offended or angry. As time went on, his slave master put him in jail with the intent that he would remain there forever. The enslavement was meant for evil, but God meant it for good. He wanted to use Joseph to save his own family. What if Joseph had let all of the bad things that people had done to him cause him to be offended? Even though it was God's plan to use Joseph to rescue his brothers, He would not have been able to use Joseph if he had allowed himself to become offended and angry.

John Bevere, a best-selling Christian author and popular conference speaker, writes in his book, The Bait of Satan, that we become offended with our friends and family (biological or Christian), not with those who we know are our enemies. He goes on to say that only those whom you care about can hurt you in that way. What a trick of the devil! The ones we love the most are the ones that he wants us to detach from and hate. As we mature spiritually we will come to a place of peace with people so that no offense will be able to take root and grow.

Unforgiveness

This is another area where we can become ensnared by the tricks of Satan. How can we be like Christ if we cannot forgive our friends not to mention our enemies? Satan really loves this one. If you want Satan to take people by the neck and really beat them up, just refuse to forgive them. When we mature in Christ, we realize that we would not be saved if Jesus had not forgiven all of us. For that reason alone, we should never want to remain in a state of unforgiveness toward anyone.

Refusing to be merciful

It is interesting to note how many Christians want to be shown mercy, but they do not want to give it. If we do not show mercy to people, then we force God to do it. We all know that Satan desires to take away any opportunity of showing mercy to anyone. If we want mercy refused to a person, Satan will be absolutely delighted to kill and destroy them. This is not what the Lord has in mind. So when someone refuses to show mercy to another, God steps in and shows them the mercy they so desperately need. As we really mature, we will not want to see anything bad happen to anyone—be they friend or foe.

SUMMARY

It is quite evident that the Lord wants us to mature in Him. Too often we, as believers, have worn clothes that were too big for us and have tried to fill shoes that were twice our normal size. It's not that the clothes and the shoes didn't belong to us; they did, but it wasn't time to wear them.

Prayerfully as you have taken the time to read this book, you have seen exactly where you stand as you make your way toward Spiritual Maturity. It is so vitally important that every believer takes inventory of his or her spiritual development, makes the necessary adjustments, and continues on to spiritual adulthood. What would become of us if we remained spiritual infants? If we did, how would we survive? How would the glory of God fill the earth? How would the glorious gospel of Jesus Christ travel throughout the entire world? Undoubtedly, we cannot afford to remain babies in Christ.

Grow up in the Lord! Mature in the things of God! Become spiritual giants in the earth! Become the manifested sons of God the creation has been expectantly waiting for!

ADDITIONAL QUOTATIONS

Maturity

A weak person is injured by prosperity; a finer person by adversity; but the finest by neither.

PAUL FROST (1938–)

God gives you and me the lumber of our lives, and offers to help us build from it a cathedral of love and praise.

JOHN POWELL

God offers a tough love that turns us into sweeter and stronger persons.

ROBERT HAROLD SCHULLER (1926–)

Has any man ever attained to inner harmony by pondering the experience of others? Not since the world began! He must pass through the fire.

NORMAN DOUGLAS (1868–1952)

If only I may grow
firmer
simpler
quieter
warmer

DAG HAMMARSKJOLD (1905–1961)

If you are born of God; then in you God will green;
His godhead is your sap; your beauty is in him.

ANGELUS SILESIUS (1624–1677)

Maturity: among other things—not to hide one's strength out of fear and, consequently, live below one's best.

DAG HAMMARSKJOLD (1905–1961)

Maturity: releasing a dream; allowing a child space to grow up; letting a friend have the freedom to be and to do.

CHARLES R. SWINDOLL (1934–)

Receive every inward and outward trouble, every disappointment, pain, uneasiness, temptation, darkness, and desolation, with both thy hands, as a true opportunity and blessed occasion of dying to self, and entering into a fuller fellowship with thy self denying, suffering Savior. Look at no inward or outward trouble in any other view; reject every other thought about it, and then every kind of trial and distress will become the blessed day of thy prosperity. That state is best, which exerciseth the highest faith in and fullest resignation to God.

WILLIAM LAW (1686–1761)

The flowering of the person is not a state at which we arrive, it is the movement that results from perpetual incompleteness.

PAUL TOURNIER (1898–1986)

The mature believer is a searching believer.

JOHN POWELL

The soul's dark cottage, batter'd and decay'd,
Lets in new light through chinks that Time hath made
Stronger by weakness; wiser men become
As they draw near to their eternal home.

EDMUND WALLER (1606–1687)

The spheres God brings us into are not meant to teach us something but to make us something.

OSWALD CHAMBERS (1874–1917)

The stronger and deeper the roots, the less visible they are.

CHARLES R. SWINDOLL (1934–)

There is no formula to teach us how to arrive at maturity, and there is no grammar for the language of the inner life.

DAG HAMMARSKJOLD (1905–1961)

Spirituality

A spirituality that preaches resignation under official brutalities, servile acquiescence in frustration and sterility, and total submission to organized injustice is one which has lost interest in holiness and remains concerned only with a spurious notion of "order."

THOMAS MERTON (1915–1968)

Every advance in spiritual life has its corresponding dangers; every step that we rise nearer God increases the depths of the gulf into which we may fall.

ROBERT H. BENSON (1871–1914)

If our spiritual life does not grow where we are, it will grow nowhere.

OSWALD CHAMBERS (1874–1917)

If you had any idea how much inward peace you would gain for yourself, and how much joy you would bring to others, by devoting yourself single-heartedly to God, you would certainly pay more attention to your spiritual progress.

THOMAS À KEMPIS (C. 1380–1471)

It is a bad thing to be satisfied spiritually.

OSWALD CHAMBERS (1874–1917)

It is right that you should begin again every day. There is no better way to finish the spiritual life than to be ever beginning.

SAINT FRANCIS OF SALES (1567–1622)

Live close to Me, and I will minister to you in secret and

do a deep inner work veiled to the eye of man. Others may view the results, but the process will be secret.

FRANCES J. ROBERTS

Spiritual rose bushes are not like natural rose bushes; with these lat- ter the thorns remain but the roses pass, with the former the thorns pass and the roses remain.

SAINT FRANCIS OF SALES (1567–1622)

We often put a false barrier between what we call the secular and the sacred, limiting the way that God can touch us and express him- self through us.

TIM HANSEL

What we call crises, God ignores; and what God reveals as the great critical moments of a man's life, we look on as humdrum common- places. When we become spiritual, we discern that God was in the humdrum commonplace and we never knew it.

OSWALD CHAMBERS (1874–1917)

When a little child becomes conscious of being a little child, the childlikeness is gone; and when a saint becomes conscious of being a saint, something has gone wrong.

OSWALD CHAMBERS (1874–1917)

CHARTS and SURVEYS

Spiritual Maturity Survey
Spiritual Maturity Survey Key
Spiritual Levels chart
Age Points Data chart
Spiritual Age and Points chart
Representative Pie chart
Spiritual Age Compilation chart
Years Saved/Spiritual Age chart

The Spiritual Maturity Survey

The Spiritual Maturity Survey is designed to ask questions based upon scriptures that are included in the discussion of the different spiritual growth levels as discussed earlier.

The questions require an answer ranging from 0-4. The first questions are from the "baby" category, the second set of questions that follow are from the "young children" category, and so on. The more questions that are answered, the more mature one is since all of the questions are based upon the requirements for spiritual maturity. At the end of the survey, a key has been provided that will allow persons to locate their position in one of the five available categories of the Spiritual Level Chart.

Spiritual Maturity Survey

Please answer the questions with a number of 0-4 in the following format:

0. **None of the time**
1. **Rarely**
2. **Some of the time**
3. **Most of the time**
4. **All of the time**

Please answer all questions to the best of your ability. Any unanswered questions will be counted as a " 0. None of the time" answers.

1. How often do you recognize the voice of God? _____ This applies to the way God speaks to you. For example, sensing His will, hearing Him speak to your mind or heart, revelation from the scriptures, etc.

2. How often do you attend Bible study? _____.

3. How often do you attend Sunday school? _____.

4. How often do you attend Sunday service? _____.

5. Do you believe that what God asks you to do is always for your good? _____.

6. Do you believe that what God asks you to do is always for His kingdom? _____.

UNDERSTANDING SPIRITUAL MATURITY

7. How well do you believe that you have overcome any sinful habit in your life? _____.

8. How often do you believe you interact intimately with the Lord during your personal prayer time? _____.

9. How often do you feel that you need not discuss the solutions to other people's problems (spiritual, physical, emotional, or natural) with neighbors, family, friends or prayer partners? _____.

10. How often do you thank the Lord for the good things that He has done for you or others? _____.

11. How often do you thank the Lord for the unhappy things that happen to you? _____.

12. How often do you thank the Lord for the bad things that other people do to you? _____.

13. How often do you try to bring the light of Jesus into situations in your life? _____.

14. Do you agree that ignorance of the Word of God no longer interferes or prevents you from making wise choices? _____.

15. How often do you believe that it is necessary to suffer for Christ's sake? _____.

16. How often do you reason that your suffering or pain at the hand of other people is not their fault? _____.

17. How often do you forgive people who hurt you intentionally in word or deed? _____.

18. How often do you rely on the Word of God to aid you or to help you get through the day? _____.

19. How often are you willing to speak the truth in love to other people? _____.

20. How often are you willing to speak the truth in love to yourself? _____.

21. Do you disagree with people who say negative things about family and friends as jokes and fun? _____.

22. How often do you try to live by example rather than by the words that you speak to people? _____.

23. Do you believe that Christian leaders should be servants of the people under their care? _____.

24. How often do you believe that you are able to recognize the tricks of the devil? _____.

25. Do you agree that Christians should not get angry with people who deserve it? _____.

26. How often do you believe that sin should be exposed? _____.

27. How often do you consider what Jesus would do in your decision making process? _____.

28. How often do you believe that you understand and follow the will of God in you life experiences? _____.

29. How often do you not make decisions based on your under- standing of a matter? _____.

30. Do you agree that in your heart the things that you have accomplished in your life (education, jobs, careers, positions of power, etc.) are the least important? _____.

31. How often do you trust God and not people (relatives, friends, spouse, boss, etc.) to get something done? _____.

32. How often do you believe that you are led by the Holy Spirit in your daily activities? _____.

33. How often do you believe that you deal with people who love you in love? _____.

34. How often do you believe that you deal with people who hate you in love? _____.

35. How often are you able to separate yourself from the things of this world that captivated you before you were saved by Jesus Christ? _____.

36. Do you have personal prayer time every day? _____.

37. Do you study your Bible every day? _____.

38. How often do you think about being holy because God is holy? _____.

39. Do you disagree that some sins are too hard to overcome, therefore God understands? _____.

40. Do you agree that you are not able to get things done by yourself spiritually and naturally? _____.

Spiritual Maturity Survey Key

1. Add up all of your answers according to the answer format.

2. Use the following key to determine your spiritual level.

0- 32 Babies
33-64 Young Children
65-96 Young Men
97-128 Young Adults
129-160 Mature Adults (Fathers)

3. Match your findings against the Spiritual Levels Chart provided.

Spiritual Levels Chart

Spiritual Level	Spiritual Age	Spiritual Emphasis	Spiritual Success	Spiritual Failure
1 Babies 0-32 Points	0-1 years * Self is alive—Functions as a mature adult in the natural * Learning to let go of self and to trust God	* Satisfying basic spiritual needs * Feeds on milk * Focused on themselves * Exercises their faith for their own benefit	* Trusts church leadership * Trusts themselves * Trusts their salvation	* Lacks knowledge of good and evil * Unskillful in the word * Major struggles with the flesh
2 Young Children 33-64 Points	1-2 years * Self less alive—Functions as a young adult in the natural * Learning to submit to the leading of the Holy Spirit	* Makes spiritual choices * Attentive to personal and public Bible study * Exercises their faith for their own benefit	* Ability to set goals to overcome some of the struggles of the flesh * Forming good Bible study habits	* Lacks understanding of the Bible knowledge that they have received * Easy prey for deception
3 Young Men (Adolescents and Teenagers) 65-96 Points	2-4 years * Dying to self in a great measure—Functions as an adolescent or teenager in the natural) *Transitioning trust from self to God	* Begins to practice biblical principles * Exercises their faith for Christ and then for themselves	* Strong in character * Devotion to Christ * Devotion to family, personal matters and church	* Struggles with self identity in Christ * Struggles with submission to authority * Struggles with transition to the next level
4 Young Adults 97-128 Points	4-10 years * Self almost completely dead —Functions as a young child in the natural * Trust the leading of the Holy Spirit more than self	* Puts more trust in God than in people * Exercises their faith for Christ and for the benefit of others * Actively seeking God's will for their lives	* Operates as a servant of the Lord * Flees from youth lust * The Word of God abides in them	* Struggles with speaking the truth in love * Struggles with more frequent spiritual battles
5 Mature Adults (Fathers) 129-160 Points	10-20 years * Self completely dead —Functions as a baby in the natural) * Does not trust self at all— Follows the leading of the Holy Spirit most of the time	* Exercises faith for Christ and for the benefit of others * Counts all worldly accomplishments as loss * Rarely focuses on self-led by the Holy Spirit * Integrity	* Walks in love on all occasions * Has an intimate relationship with Christ * Reproduces themselves often *Walks in the power of His resurrection * The will of God is paramount	* Zealousness for church work may cause compromise of intimate time with Christ * Struggles with wanting more for their sons than they want for themselves

The Age Points Data Chart

The Age Points Data Chart calculates the points of every age by month from age one (1) month to two hundred forty (240) months or twenty years of growth. This chart indicates that babies and young children in Christ will receive 2.7 points for every month of growth for the first two years of their spiritual life, young men receive 1.3 points for each month, young adults receive .430556 points for each month, and mature adults receive .258333 points for each month.

Notice that this chart indicates that babies and young children grow very fast. Just as in the natural, they learn and grow fast in the first two years. As a person gets older in the spiritual things, however, he or she grows at a slower rate, which is also true of natural growth.

The Age Points Data chart shows that many people may only be a fraction of a point apart and will receive the same whole number as another even though they may be a few months apart in their score. This happens because of the slowness of growth at this age. Each calculation reflects a slow but sure process of spiritual growth. Because of these calculations, I have also provided another chart, The Spiritual Age Points Data Chart, to express whole numbers. The Spiritual Age Points Data Chart is also used to assign spiritual age.

Age Points Data

Babies — Young Children — Young Men

Babies & Young Children (2.7 Points per month)		Young Men (1.3 Points per Month)	
1	2.7	2.1	65.3
2	5.3	2.2	66.6
3	7.9	2.3	67.9
4	10.6	2.4	69.2
5	13.3	2.5	70.5
6	16	2.6	71.8
7	18.7	2.7	73.1
8	21.4	2.8	74.4
9	24.1	2.9	75.7
10	26.8	2.1	77
11	29.5	2.11	78.3
1 Yr	32	3 Yrs	80.9
1.1	34.7	3.1	82.2
1.2	37.4	3.2	83.5
1.3	40.1	3.3	84.8
1.4	42.8	3.4	86.1
1.5	45.5	3.5	87.4
1.6	48.2	3.6	88.7
1.7	50.9	3.7	90
1.8	53.6	3.8	91.3
1.9	56.3	3.9	92.6
1.1	59	3.1	93.9
1.11	61.7	3.11	95.2
2 Yrs	64	4 Yrs	97

Young Adults

5.166667 per year
0.430556 per month

4.1	97.043	6.1	107.376344	8.1	117.7098
4.2	97.473556	6.2	107.8069	8.3	118.1403
4.3	97.904112	6.3	108.237456	8.3	118.5709
4.4	98.334668	6.4	108.668012	8.4	119.0015
4.5	98.765224	6.5	109.098568	8.5	119.432
4.6	99.19578	6.6	109.529124	8.6	119.8626
4.7	99.626336	6.7	109.95968	8.7	120.2931
4.8	100.056892	6.8	110.390236	8.8	120.7237
4.9	100.487448	6.9	110.820792	8.9	121.1542
4.1	100.918004	6.1	111.251348	8.1	121.5848
4.11	101.34856	6.11	111.681904	8.11	122.0153
5 Yrs	101.779116	7 Yrs	112.1125596	9 Yrs	122.4459
5.1	102.209672	7.1	112.5431156	9.1	122.8765
5.2	102.640228	7.2	112.9736716	9.2	123.307
5.3	103.070784	7.3	113.4042276	9.3	123.7376
5.4	103.50134	7.4	113.8347836	9.4	124.1681
5.5	103.931896	7.5	114.2653396	9.5	124.5987
5.6	104.362452	7.6	114.6958956	9.6	125.0292
5.7	104.793008	7.7	115.1264516	9.7	125.4598
5.8	105.223564	7.8	115.5570076	9.8	125.8904
5.9	105.65412	7.9	115.9875636	9.9	126.3209
5.1	106.084676	7.1	116.4181196	9.1	126.7515
5.11	106.515232	7.11	116.8486756	9.11	127.182
6 Yrs	106.945788	8 Yrs	117.2792316	10 Yrs	127.6126

Mature Adults

3.1 per year
0.258333 per month

10.1	127.8746	12.1	134.0746	14.1	140.274633
10.2	128.133	12.2	134.333	14.2	140.532966
10.3	128.3913	12.3	134.5913	14.3	140.791299
10.4	128.6496	12.4	134.8496	14.4	141.049632
10.5	128.908	12.5	135.108	14.5	141.307965
10.6	129.1663	12.6	135.3663	14.6	141.566298
10.7	129.4246	12.7	135.6246	14.7	141.824631
10.8	129.683	12.8	135.883	14.8	142.082964
10.9	129.9413	12.9	136.1413	14.9	142.341297
10.1	130.1996	12.1	136.3996	14.1	142.59963
10.11	130.458	12.11	136.658	14.11	142.857963
11 Yrs	130.7163	13 Yrs	136.9163	15 Yrs	143.116296
11.1	130.9746	13.1	137.1746	15.1	143.374629
11.2	131.233	13.2	137.433	15.2	143.632962
11.3	131.4913	13.3	137.6913	15.3	143.891295
11.4	131.7496	13.4	137.9496	15.4	144.149628
11.5	132.008	13.5	138.208	15.5	144.407961
11.6	132.2663	13.6	138.4663	15.6	144.666294
11.7	132.5246	13.7	138.7246	15.7	144.924627
11.8	132.783	13.8	138.983	15.8	145.18296
11.9	133.0413	13.9	139.2413	15.9	145.441293
11.1	133.2996	13.1	139.4996	15.1	145.699626
11.11	133.558	13.11	139.758	15.11	145.957959
12 Yrs	133.8163	14 Yrs	140.0163	16 Years	146.216292

Mature Adults

3.1   per year
0.258333   per month

16.1	146.474625	18.1	152.674617
16.2	146.732958	18.2	152.93295
16.3	146.991291	18.3	153.191283
16.4	147.249624	18.4	153.449616
16.5	147.507957	18.5	153.707949
16.6	147.76629	18.6	153.966282
16.7	148.024623	18.7	154.224615
16.8	148.282956	18.8	154.482948
16.9	148.541289	18.9	154.741281
16.1	148.799622	18.1	154.999614
16.11	149.057955	18.11	155.257947
17 Yrs	149.316288	19 Yrs	155.51628
17.1	149.574621	19.1	155.774613
17.2	149.832954	19.2	156.032946
17.3	150.091287	19.3	156.291279
17.4	150.34962	19.4	156.549612
17.5	150.607953	19.5	156.807945
17.6	150.866286	19.6	157.066278
17.7	151.124619	19.7	157.324611
17.8	151.382952	19.8	157.582944
17.9	151.641285	19.9	157.841277
17.1	151.899618	19.1	158.09961
17.11	152.157951	19.11	158.357943
18 Yrs	152.416284	20 Yrs	158.616276

Spiritual Age And Points Chart

Babies—0-32 Points [0-1 Year]

Months/Year	1	2	3	4	5	6	7	8	9	10	11	12
Points	2	5	7	10	13	16	18	21	24	26	29	32

Young Children—33-64 Points [1-2 Years]

Years/Months	1.1	1.2	1.3	1.4	1.5	1.6	1.7	1.8	1.9	1.10	1.11	2
Points	34	37	40	42	45	48	50	53	56	59	61	64

Young Men—65-96 Points [2-4 Years] (Adolescence and Teenagers)

Years/Months	2.1	2.2	2.3	2.4	2.5	2.6	2.7	2.8	2.9	2.10	2.11	3
Points	65	66	67	69	70	71	73	74	75	77	73	81
Years/Months	3.1	3.2	3.3	3.4	3.5	3.6	3.7	3.8	3.9	3.10	3.11	4
Points	82	83	84	86	87	88	90	91	92	93	95	97

Young Adults—97-128 Points [4-10 Years]

Years/Months	4.1	4.2	4.3	4.4	4.5	4.6	4.7	4.8	4.9	4.10	4.11	5
Points	97	97	97	98	98	99	99	100	100	100	101	101
Years/Months	5.1	5.2	5.3	5.4	5.5	5.6	5.7	5.8	5.9	5.10	5.11	6
Points	102	102	103	103	103	104	104	105	105	106	106	106
Years/Months	6.1	6.2	6.3	6.4	6.5	6.6	6.7	6.8	6.9	6.10	6.11	7
Points	107	107	108	108	109	109	109	110	110	111	111	112
Years/Months	7.1	7.2	7.3	7.4	7.5	7.6	7.7	7.8	7.9	7.10	7.11	8
Points	112	112	113	113	114	114	115	115	115	116	116	117
Years/Months	8.1	8.2	8.3	8.4	8.5	8.6	8.7	8.8	8.9	8.10	8.11	9
Points	117	118	118	119	119	119	120	120	121	121	122	122
Years/Months	9.1	9.2	9.3	9.4	9.5	9.6	9.7	9.8	9.9	9.10	9.11	10
Points	122	123	123	124	124	125	125	125	126	126	127	127

UNDERSTANDING SPIRITUAL MATURITY

Mature Adults (Fathers)—129-160 Points [10-20 Years]

Years/Months	10.1	10.2	10.3	10.4	10.5	10.6	10.7	10.8	10.9	10.10	10.11	11
Points	127	128	128	128	128	129	129	129	129	130	130	130
Years/Months	11.1	11.2	11.3	11.4	11.5	11.6	11.7	11.8	11.9	11.10	11.11	12
Points	130	131	131	131	132	132	132	132	133	133	133	133
Years/Months	12.1	12.2	12.3	12.4	12.5	12.6	12.7	12.8	12.9	12.10	12.11	13
Points	134	134	134	134	135	135	135	135	136	136	136	136
Years/Months	13.1	13.2	13.3	13.4	13.5	13.6	13.7	13.8	13.9	13.10	13.11	14
Points	137	137	137	137	138	138	138	138	139	139	139	140
Years/Months	14.1	14.2	14.3	14.4	14.5	14.6	14.7	14.8	14.9	14.10	14.11	15
Point	140	140	140	141	141	141	141	142	142	142	142	143
Years/Months	15.1	15.2	15.3	15.4	15.5	15.6	15.7	15.8	15.9	15.10	15.11	16
Points	143	143	143	144	144	144	144	145	145	145	145	146
Years/Months	16.1	16.2	16.3	16.4	16.5	16.6	16.7	16.8	16.9	16.10	16.11	17
Points	146	146	146	147	147	147	148	148	148	148	149	149
Years/Months	17.1	17.2	17.3	17.4	17.5	17.6	17.7	17.8	17.9	17.10	17.11	18
Points	149	149	150	150	150	150	151	151	151	151	152	152
Years/Months	18.1	18.2	18.3	18.4	18.5	18.6	18.7	18.8	18.9	18.10	18.11	19
Points	152	152	153	153	153	153	154	154	154	154	155	155
Years/Months	19.1	19.2	19.3	19.4	19.5	19.6	19.7	19.8	19.9	19.10	19.11	20
Points	155	156	156	156	156	157	157	157	157	158	158	158

The Representative Pie Chart

This pie chart represents the number of persons in each age group by color. With the exception of "babies" and "young children," the "mature adult" group is the smallest group when it should actually be the largest. The largest group appears to be the "young adult" group which should be the mature adult group based on the number of years saved. This chart clearly indicates that there are a limited number of mature adults to father the younger Christians.

Representative Pie Chart

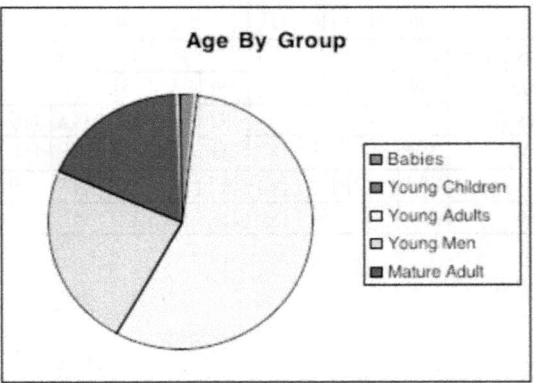

As we move from the Young Men level in our spiritual growth, the process is much slower. By now we have surrendered all the easy things to Christ and the rest takes much time and patience. I am so glad that the Lord does not get tired and impatient with us, because many of us get stuck at a particular level and do not realize that the Lord wants us to go further.

The Spiritual Age Compilation Chart

The following sister chart to the Representative Pie Chart, the Spiritual Age Compilation chart, will give us a ballpark figure of how many persons fall into each spiritual age level (up to 25 years).

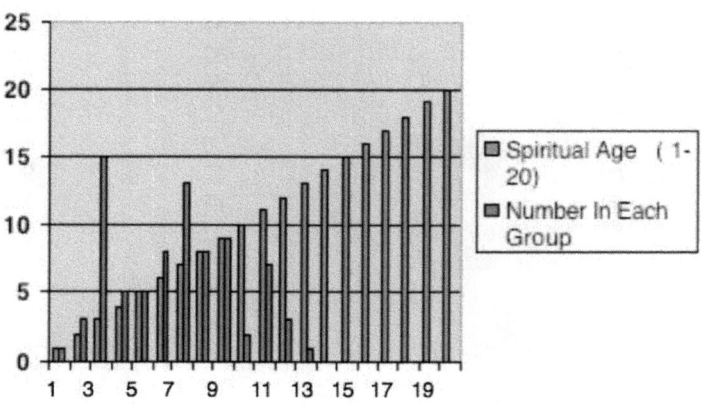

Spiritual Age Compilation

The Years Saved/Spiritual Age Chart

As we move from the "young men" level in our spiritual growth, the maturing process becomes much slower, just like the natural and biological growth process. By now we have surrendered all of the easy things to Christ, and the rest simply takes much more time and patience. We must keep in mind, though, that the number of years that we've been saved does not always indicate our level of spiritual maturity as shown in the following chart, Years Saved/Spiritual Age.

Years Saved/Spiritual Age

Natural Age	Spiritual Age	Years Saved	Survey Score
87	3	39	87
74	4	62	98
72	5	1	102
67	8	55	118
67	6	21	107
64	3	58	95
62	11	51	132
62	10	32	128
61	9	53	125
61	6	52	110
60	7	30	116
60	3	55	96
59	7	48	116
58	7	2	116
58	7	4	114
56	11	20	131
56	4	56	109
56	3	20	96
55	8	7	117
55	7	47	116
55	9	12	124
55	7	45	113
53	7	25	108
52	5	23	104
52	7	24	112
52	13	40	137
52	11	41	132
52	14	30	140
51	4	30	118
50	7	35	114
50	11	20	133
50	3	12	100
49	2	49	80
48	7	38	114
48	7	40	113
48	3	5	88
47	7	20	116
47	6	7	107

UNDERSTANDING SPIRITUAL MATURITY

Natural Age	Spiritual Age	Years Saved	Survey Score
45	11		131
45	4	36	98
43	4	33	121
42	12		134
41	9	16	125
41	4	6	116
41	3	30	94
41	4	20	118
41	14	5	140
40	4	40	107
40	3	40	91
40	12	16	134
40	12	3	136
40	14	10	142
40	4	28	101
40	11	32	132
39	9	6	124
39	11	8	131
38	3	2	88
38	13	8	139
38	6	23	110
37	3	18	85
37	9	6	123
37	4	20	97
37	3	11	94
36	6	2	109
36	13	25	139
36	8	11	119
35	8	5	120
35	3	35	86
35	2	8	92
34	2	4	70
34	8	5	122
34	5	11	105
34	3	25	87
33	9	4	125
33	3	1	85
31	3		83

Natural Age	Spiritual Age	Years Saved	Survey Score
31	4	9	118
30	13	3	139
30	3	18	81
29	5	2	103
29	10	7	129
28	3	17	92
28	9	8	123
27	2	5	92
26	9	5	125
25	6	8	108
25	5	10	104
24	7	14	112
23	8	4	121
20	3	11	85
19	9	3	124
14	2	3	66
12	3	5	81
	3		92
	3		95

ABOUT THE AUTHOR

Cynthia V. White is a native of Macon, Georgia. She is the daughter of the late Cynthia Ollie Mary Smith Turner and the late Rev. Lee A. Townes and Sallie Townes. She is a widow and the mother of six children and grandmother of nine grandchildren.

Dr. White graduated from Ballard Hudson High School in Macon, Georgia and continued her education at Morris Brown College in Atlanta, Georgia where she received a Bachelor of Science Degree in Mathematics and Education. In May 1999 she received the degree of Master of Arts in Biblical Studies of the Old Testament from Maple Springs Baptist Bible College and Seminary, Capitol Heights Maryland. In May 2002, she received her doctorate degree from the same college.

After 31 years of dedicated service, Dr. White retired from the Department of the Navy in January 1999. During her tenure there she served as the head of the Computer Aided Design and Manufacturing Department, the Industrial Improvement Technologies Department, the Joint Electronic Drawings and Manufacturing of Industrial Data Department, the Military Construction Projects Department, and she also served as the Program Manager for the Service Craft Management and Manufacturing Technology Department for the Naval Shipyards.

Dr. White is a strong supporter of community services. She has participated in fundraisers for the March of Dimes, she supports children in need programs, and is a former member of the Board of Directors for the Center for Community Development of Housing for the Mentally Ill and the Aged. Adding to her extensive resume of charitable work, Dr. White is also a former member of the Board of Directors and served as the Secretary of Bethel House, a community support center for people in need of help such as food, housing, education, jobs and the like.

During her Christian journey, Dr. White has taught in several venues to include Sunday school, Vacation Bible School, Bible study, workshops and conferences, and other Christian settings. She has also served as a member of the choir and steward board.

Currently, Dr. White serves an ordained Elder of God Is In Control Church in Waldorf, Maryland under the leadership of Bishop Elect Rodney and Elder Betty Walker. As a member and leader, she serves as Chief Elder in the Apostolic, Secretary of Church Finances, Church Administrator, as a member of the Praise and Worship team, as a member of Another Touch of Glory Covenant Ministries School of the Prophets Board of Presbyters, and as a valued member of the God Is In Control Church Ministerial/Administrative Staff and the Another Touch of Glory Covenant Ministries Staff.

Dr. Cynthia V. White is also the owner and Chief Executive Officer of a recently established business, "Fruit That Remain, LLC," a company designed to provide new businesses with structure, vision, and direction and to assist established business owners with products and services that will contribute to their success and help them accomplish the particular goals and objectives they have set forth for their business.

Above all, Apostle White is a child of the living God who has been gifted to teach the Word of God with power and demonstration, to declare the will of God with clarity and precise articulation, and to love the unloveable as Christ loves us!

CONTACT INFORMATION

To contact Dr. Cynthia V. White, please write to:

Dr. Cynthia V. White
1282 Smallwood Drive West #195
Waldorf, Maryland 20603
Phone: (301) 442-3116

other works by the author
"What Your Father Never Told You... About Business"
This booklet is designed to provoke you into thinking about some of the requirements not often discussed by others, but are essential in understand- ing the risks and the costs of operating a successful business. Each administrative key point is posed in a question format and will be beneficial before starting and going through the various life cycles of your business success.

Also available in CD format
To order additional books or CD's, please contact:
Kingdom Christian Bookstore
2778 Crain Highway
Waldorf, MD 20601
Voice: (301) 843-9267 • Fax: (301) 843-1773

BIBLIOGRAPHY

1. Ryrie, Charles Cadwell, Ryrie Study Bible Expanded Edition New International Version. Chicago: Moody, 1994.

2. Scorield, Rev. C. I., ed., The Holy Bible. New York: Oxford University Press, 1945.

3. Erikson, Millard J., Christian Theology. Grand Rapids: Baker Book House, 1985.

4. Bright, Bill, A Handbook for Christian Maturity. Orlando, FL: Newlife Publications, 1994.

5. Sanders, J. Oswald, Spiritual Maturity. Chicago: Moody Press, 1994.

6. Sanders, J. Oswald, Spiritual Leadership. Chicago: Moody Press, 1994.

7. Sanders, J. Oswald, Spiritual Discipleship. Chicago: Moody Press, 1994.

8. International Standard Bible Encyclopedia, Electronic Database, copyright © 1996 by Biblesoft.

9. Nelson's Illustrated Bible Dictionary, copyright © 1986, Thomas Nelson Publishers.

10. Strong, A.H., Systematic Theology (1907), p. 857; L.S. Chafer, Systematic Theology (1948), 3:242, 243; 7:9-11; J.B. Lightfoot, St. Paul's Epistle to the Galatians (1966), pp. 168-69; C. E.B. Cranfield, A Critical and Exegetical Commentary on the Epistle to the Romans, International Critical Commentary (1975), 1:396-98; F.F. Bruce, Epistle to the Galatians, New International Greek Testament Commentary (1982), pp. 196-98.from New Unger's Bible Dictionary.

11. New Unger's Bible Dictionary, originally published by Moody Press of Chicago, Illinois. Copyright (C) 1988.)

12. Gill,JohnD.D.,ExpositionOfTheOldAndNewTestaments.Vol.9,Paris,

13. Barnes, Albert, Notes On The New Testament. Grand Rapids: Baker Book House, 1884-85.

14. Catholic Encyclopedia, copyright © 1913 by the Encyclopedia Press, Inc. Electronic version copyright © 1997 by New Advent Inc.

15. Berry, Stephen R., Sons of God. St. Louis, MO: PCA Historical Center, 1974.

16. Barron, J., Robert. Brubaker, Omar, Clark, Robert E., Understanding People: Children, Youth, Adults. Wheaton, Illinois: Evangelical Training Association, 1989.

17. Edersheim, Alfred, The Life and Times of Jesus the Messiah. Peabody: Henderson Publishers, 1993.

18. Nee, Watchman, Spiritual Authority. New York: Christian Fellowship Publishing, 1972.

19. Wilke, Lori, Requirements for Greatness—Justice, Mercy and Humility. Shippensburg, PA: Destiny Image, 1996.

20. Hamon, Bill. Apostles, Prophets and the Coming Moves of God. Santa Rosa Beach, FL: 1997.

21. Conner, Kevin J., The Church In the New Testament. Kent England: Sovereign World International and Portland, Oregon: BT Publishing. 1982.
22. Conner, Kevin J., The Foundations of Christian Doctrine—A Practical Guide to Christian Belief. Kent England:

Sovereign World International and Portland, Oregon: City Bible Publishing. 1980.

23. Stanley, Charles, The Wonderful Spirit Filled Life. Nashville, Atlanta, London, Vancouver: Thomas Nelson Publishers, 1992.

24. Ryrie, Charles C., Balancing The Christian Life. Chicago: The Moody Bible Institute, 1994.

25. Robinson, Haddon, Decision Making By The Book—How To Choose Wisely In An Age Of Options. United States Canada England: Victor Books, 1984.

26. Hanby, Mark, You Have Not Many Fathers—Recovering the Generational Blessing. Shippensburg, Pennsylvania: Destiny Image Publishers. 1997.

27. Riffel, Herman, Growing in Christian Maturity Shippensburg, PA: Destiny Image Publishers, Inc., 1997.

28. Stanford, Miles J., Principles of Spiritual Growth. Lincoln, Nebraska: Back to the Bible, 1997.

29. Warfield, B. B., The Person and Work of Christ (1950), pp. 325-50.

30. Morris, L. L., The Cross in the New Testament (1964), The Apostolic Preaching of the Cross (1965).

31. Bootzin, Richard R., Acocella, Joan Ross, Alloy, Lauren B. Abnormal Psychology Current Perspectives: New York, McGraw Hill, Inc., 1993.

32. Draper's Book of Quotations for the Christian World, Parsons Technology, 1997.

NOTES

1. Oswald Sanders, *Spiritual Maturity*. Chicago: Moody Press, 1994.

2. Miles J. Stanford, *Principles of Spiritual Growth*. Lincoln, Nebraska: Back to the Bible, 1997.

3. *Draper's Book of Quotations for the Christian World*, Parsons Technology, 1997.

4. *Draper's Book of Quotations for the Christian World*, Parsons Technology, 1997.

5. Kevin J. Conner, *The Foundations of Christian Doctrine—A Practical Guide to Christian Belief*. Kent England: Sovereign World International and Portland, Oregon: City Bible Publishing. 1980.

6. Oswald Sanders, *Spiritual Leadership*. Chicago: Moody Press, 1994.

7. Mark Hamby, *You Have Not Many Fathers—Recovering the Generational Blessing*. Shippensburg, Penn.: Destiny Image Publishers, 1997.

8. Herman Riffel, *Growing in Christian Maturity*. Shippensburg, Penn.: Destiny Image Publishers, Inc., 1997.

9. Millard J. Erikson, *Christian Theology*. Grand Rapids: Baker Book House, 1985.

10. *International Standard Bible Encyclopedia*, Electronic Database, copyright by Biblesoft, 1996.

11. Haddon Robinson, *Decision Making By The Book—How To Choose Wisely In An Age Of Options*. United States Canada England: Victor Books, 1984.

12. Bill Bright, *A Handbook for Christian Maturity*. Orlando, Florida: Newlife Publications, 1994.

13. Barron, J., Robert. Brubaker, Omar, Clark, Robert E., *Understanding People: Children, Youth, Adults*. Wheaton, Illinois: Evangelical Training Association, 1989.

14. Robert Barron, J. Omar Brubaker, Robert E. Clark, *Understanding People: Children, Youth, Adults*. Wheaton, Illinois: Evangelical Training Association, 1989.

15. Richard R. Bootzin, Joan Ross Acocella, Lauren B. Alloy. *Abnormal Psychology Current Perspectives*. New York: McGraw Hill, Inc., 1993.

16. Robert Barron, J. Omar Brubaker, Robert E. Clark, *Understanding People: Children, Youth, Adults*. Wheaton, Illinois: Evangelical Training Association, 1989.

www.ingramcontent.com/pod-product-compliance
Lightning Source LLC
Chambersburg PA
CBHW071131090426
42736CB00012B/2084